THE MANAGER'S
POCKET CALCULATOR

THE MANAGER'S
POCKET CALCULATOR

A QUICK GUIDE TO ESSENTIAL
BUSINESS FORMULAS AND RATIOS

MICHAEL C. THOMSETT

AMACOM

American Management Association

New York • Atlanta • Brussels • Chicago • Mexico City • San Francisco
Shanghai • Tokyo • Toronto • Washington, D.C.

This publication is designed to provide accurate and authoritative information in regard to the subject matter covered. It is sold with the understanding that the publisher is not engaged in rendering legal, accounting, or other professional service. If legal advice or other expert assistance is required, the services of a competent professional person should be sought.

Library of Congress Cataloging-in-Publication Data

Thomsett, Michael C.
    Manager's pocket calculator : a quick guide to essential business formulas and ratios / Michael C. Thomsett.
        p.   cm.
    Includes bibliographical references and index.
    ISBN-13: 978-0-8144-1635-8
    ISBN-10: 0-8144-1635-7
    1. Business mathematics.   I. Title.
    HF5691.T483 2011
    650.01'513—dc22   2010003411

About AMA

American Management Association (www.amanet.org) is a world leader in talent development, advancing the skills of individuals to drive business success. Our mission is to support the goals of individuals and organizations through a complete range of products and services, including classroom and virtual seminars, webcasts, webinars, podcasts, conferences, corporate and government solutions, business books and research. AMA's approach to improving performance combines experiential learning—learning through doing—with opportunities for ongoing professional growth at every step of one's career journey.

Printing number

10 9 8 7 6 5 4 3 2 1

Contents

The Basic Problem with Numbers

It's all in the numbers. Everyone has heard this statement and it is true. Your performance is invariably judged by how much profit you create or by how much cost you incur in your segment, team, or department. The so-called bottom line—profit or loss—is the universal means for monitoring performance and for determining whether an initiative was worthwhile.

With the dominance of the bottom line in every aspect of how your performance is graded, you have a distinct advantage if you are skilled at conveying information in terms of profitability. Conversely, you are at a distinct *dis*advantage if you cannot communicate the profit or loss aspects of your work to management. On a most basic level, just asking management for something is less effective than demonstrating how an approval is going to create additional profits or cut costs (related directly to revenues) and expenses (overhead, not related directly to revenues). This is the rudimentary distinction between managers with communication skills and those who struggle every day trying to find the best way to communicate what they know and what they have achieved.

If you do not have background and education in finance, you probably struggle with these issues on a daily basis. Even those with training in accounting may find it difficult to summarize their requests in plain, simple, and clear terms for management. No one is immune from the difficulty in matching numerical information with a request or recommendation. For some, even if the numerical aspects of the job are comfortable, conveying their significance to management can be very difficult. For others, even those with exceptional communication skills, reducing the numbers ("crunching") to the basics is the real challenge.

Your purpose in making effective use of numerical information is to convey the essential data that management needs to make an informed decision—and to make your case convincingly. Faced with an unending array of choices, management's desire is to make choices that are not only the most profitable but that also involve the least risk. It is not enough to demonstrate that a decision is likely to be profitable if it also incurs unacceptable risks: potential liability, supply chain losses, reduced customer satisfaction, or damage to brand and reputation. When an esteemed company like Mattel contracted for its manufacturing in China but failed to properly supervise quality control, toys were sold in the United States containing harmful lead. The product cost aspects of this mistake were easily rectified. However, the reputation to the company, while less tangible, is likely to affect profits at an unknown level and for an unknown period of time. So the analysis of risk involves both tangible and intangible considerations, making it difficult to *know* how much risk is really involved in creating x profits as the result of y decisions.

What this means for you is that any communication is going to be based on an evaluation of profit and loss, many forms of risk, and the time required for return on investment, just to name a few considerations. How do you communicate the relevant facts to management? How do you reduce the research to well-supported recommendations or to caution statements? These are only a few of the issues you face in managing information and in massaging it to create an effective, simple, and honest method of communication.

This book is designed to provide the basic skills in using financial and statistical facts, whether in reports or presentations. The book's purpose is not to provide instruction in communication abilities but to demonstrate how to develop a range of formulas and how to apply them to typical situations. The information enables you to more confidently and effectively include financial and statistical data in your reports and presentations and to provide convincing arguments to support your recommendations.

Each chapter introduces a series of formulas and explains the context in which to apply them. The step-by-step formulation is followed by an example to show how the application of the formula works. Because so much of business involves money management, the first two chapters deal with the time value of money, compound interest, and present and future value. Granted, many of the calculations involved can be performed with handheld devices on online free calculators. However, these chapters enable you to express these concepts more effectively by understanding how the calculations are performed, why time creates value, and how compounding works.

Chapters 3 and 4 explain how to calculate return and breakeven points, issues that virtually every manager (even those lacking financial training) have to contend with. For many nonaccounting managers, these topics can be overwhelming and complex, making effective communication a hopeless cause. However, the formulations themselves are not at all complicated; they are simply not well explained in most applications. These chapters show you how to make the complex simple and how to create powerful communications tools by mastering their explanations.

Chapters 5 through 7 focus on financial reporting, normally the realm of accountants. Why is this area important to you? For nonfinancial managers, the mysterious and complex methods of financial analysis makes communication difficult between managers and their audience. The skills needed to understand and explain financial reports are not really at all difficult; they simply need to be placed in context. This is especially true for topics such as depreciation and how it affects financial reports on a noncash basis.

Chapters 8, 9, and 10 explore the preparation and organization of reports, budgets, and forecasts. Virtually every manager is required to prepare reports, create departmental budgets, or forecast future revenues. Many dread the experience. The tasks are not only numerically complex, but they may also be political minefields within the organization. These chapters explain how to incorporate numerical information into reports, not as necessary evils that can destroy an otherwise effective presentation, but as the means to support strong arguments and *improve* how information is conveyed. The dreaded budget and forecast are explored with the same premise: Once you master the communication of the numbers, all your presentations (especially budgets and forecasts) become more effective and useful.

Chapter 11 demonstrates how to best use statistics, especially in reports. Most people dread statistics because they are complex. In this chapter, you see how the effective use of statistics can reduce pages of complex calculations to a declarative sentence, as well as how to use numbers to support conclusions rather than obscuring the facts. The effective use of statistics creates insights among the audience for your reports, rather than the glazed-over eyes so often seen while presenters go through the numbers.

Finally, Chapter 12 goes through a few effective and intriguing math shortcuts. These are useful in developing your mastery of numbers, and they reduce the time required for mental calculation. Math may not always be an enjoyable exercise for those who struggle with it, but these shortcuts make the process more manageable. They show you how to convert a struggle into a series of rewarding exercises with satisfying results.

At the conclusion of the book, all of the formulas are summarized in alphabetical order for easy reference. This format complements the organization of the book. Within each chapter, the discussion is always based on context, followed by a formula, and concluded with an example. The set of formulas, grouped in the appendix, helps you to reference the many formulas in one place.

The purpose in preparing this book is to provide alternative methods for reports, budgets, and other numerical chores to increase their effectiveness and facilitate their communication. The perception that a background in finance gives some managers an advantage over others is based on a reality: Training and experience pay off. This book arms you with communication skills designed to improve your reports and presentations. Once you master the numerical aspects of your message, your overall communication skills rise and your effectiveness improves as a direct result.

NOTATION USED IN THIS BOOK

An effort has been made to maintain a layman's version of mathematical functions. So the standard symbols for basic functions are used in all formulas:

+	addition
−	subtraction
+(−)	addition or subtraction
×	multiplication
÷	division

Symbols used for basic functions on spreadsheets conform to the Excel formatting, which uses the symbols, +, −, *, and / for the four functions.

Superscripting is used to indicate multiples of a value. So n^2 is the direction for squaring n. In formulas requiring many more functions than squaring, the superscripted value is either shown or marked as an unknown number like n^x, with x representing a variable. Subscripting is used to distinguish values from one another in a series of different values. So when you see n_1 and n_2 you know that there are two different versions of n.

Parentheses are used in formulas when different functions have to be separated. For example, the instruction $a + b \div c$ can have two different meanings, depending on which operation is separated. So $(a + b) \div c$ is not the same as $a + (b \div c)$.

Other mathematical expressions in use are the square root symbol ($\sqrt{}$) and two Greek symbols used in some mathematical functions: lowercase sigma (σ) and pi (π). In one instance, a symbol has been use to indicate affixing one value to another, using a colon. If you are to affix y to x, it is shown as $x{:}y$. In other words, rather than being added, an affixed value is added to the end of the preceding number. For example, *adding* 25 to 700 creates the answer 725. *Affixing* 25 to 700 (700:25) creates the result 70,025 and is shown in formulation as *700:25*.

The use of these shortcut symbols has been held to a minimum on the assumption that most managers prefer to avoid higher mathematical formulas or explanations that assume too much math training or knowledge.

The Manager's Pocket Calculator

CHAPTER 1

Compound Interest: The *Power* of Money

M oney and time are directly and inescapably related. The longer money is left on deposit, the more it earns; similarly, the longer it takes to repay a loan, the more it costs. Although this concept—that the benefit or cost of money increases over time—is easily explained, it is not always understood. This chapter explains how the time value of money works and provides formulas for calculating interest in various ways.

In the calculation of interest cost, time is the most critical element, even more so than the rate. These two factors—time and rate—define the true cost of money. When an organization borrows money through working capital loans, equipment financing, or any other vehicle, there is a tendency to focus on the interest rate only. Though the rate is important, there is more to consider, including the monthly payment required and the length of time it is going to take to retire the loan. At 7.5%, for example, a 10-year repayment is going to cost twice as much in interest as a loan for the same amount with a four-year repayment.

▶ Example: You borrow $20,000 from your local lender. You have a choice: repayment in four years at $483.58 per month or repayment in eight years at $277.68 per month. Your first reaction is that the lower payment is desirable. However, when you add up your total of payments for each of these loans, you discover the truth: The total for the four-year term is $23,211.84 (48 months × $483.58), and the total for the eight-year term is $26,657.28 (96 months × $277.68). The difference in total interest is $3,445.44. The interest cost for the longer-term loan is twice as much as for the shorter-term loan.

Selecting a repayment period is a matter of balance between the affordability of the monthly payment and the overall cost of interest. This decision is the essence of the time value of money. So in calculating the cost of repayment for this $20,000 loan, you need to evaluate the interest rate and monthly payment; however, you also need to compare the total cost of interest based on different loan repayment terms.

In addition to the monthly payment and overall interest cost, the method of interest calculation affects the total of payments as well. You need to employ different interest compounding methods, not to mention calculating the cost of borrowing money, for various reporting and budgeting purposes.

TIME VALUE OF MONEY: THE CONCEPT

A combination of elements defines the true cost or benefit of money. The cost is incurred when you borrow and the benefit results from savings. There are four elements:

1. Amount borrowed
2. Repayment term
3. Interest rate
4. Compounding method

1. Amount Borrowed

The most easily understood element of all is the amount borrowed. Most people understand that the more money they borrow, the higher the repayment is going to be. This simplicity is obscured, however, by the varying payment levels for different lengths of repayment.

➤ Example: At 7.5%, a $20,000 loan requires monthly payments of $483.58 over four years. However, you can borrow $30,000 and pay only $416.52 per month or *less* in monthly payments. The drawback, however, is that repayment of the $30,000 will take eight years, and the total interest is $9,985.92. (The $9,985.92 is almost equal to the additional amount borrowed: $30,000 − $20,000). The smaller loan with faster repayment costs $3,211.84, or interest equal to about one-third of the longer-term loan with smaller payments.

Which loan is better suited to your needs? For most business owners and managers, the commitment to debt service that is twice the length of the original $20,000 loan has to be a primary consideration. The amount borrowed is $10,000 more, but you are committed to repayments for twice as many years.

Developing a rationale to justify the lengthier borrowing schedule is possible.

➤ Example: If you originally wanted only $20,000, why not borrow $30,000 and invest the difference? The payments are about the same amount, but the $10,000 is enough to repay all of the interest on the higher loan.

This argument overlooks two important facts, however. First, although the higher loan amount creates enough cash to pay the interest, you also have to repay the additional $10,000 borrowed, and that translates to twice the length of repayment. Second, will you really save the difference? As many business managers have realized, setting up a reserve and leaving it in place is difficult. Over time, management is going to be tempted to use the fund for other necessities, and ultimately the end result is the same: The longer-term loan is going to be more expensive and require a lengthier repayment commitment.

2. Repayment Term

Picking a repayment term should never be based on the monthly payment alone; it should include an analysis of cash flow requirements and limitations (see Chapter 4), as well as the affordability of borrowing. You may want to borrow money for any number of reasons, but all should be analyzed with a series of key questions:

- Can I afford the repayments?
- How does a loan affect my cash flow?
- Have I identified how the loan will increase profits? (Profitability can be affected by expanded markets, greater efficiencies, or improved products or services.)

   The repayment term might seem like a no-brainer: You want to get a loan repaid as quickly as you can afford, at the lowest interest cost, and with the least impact on cash flow. However, the question also has to depend on affordability and cash flow, not merely on the concept that "more is good" when it comes to adding debt. This common belief can not only be destructive to your ability to fund repayments while maintaining cash flow, but it can also ignore how much negative impact debt might have on future expansion and profits.

3. Interest Rate

The interest rate you are required to pay to borrow money (or that you are paid to save or invest) makes a tremendous difference over time. Some loans can be negotiated for a lower interest rate in exchange for more rapid repayment, saving money over the full term. For example, the difference between 7.0% and 7.5% is about $5.19 per month over 10 years. For a $20,000 loan, that comes out to a difference of $622.80. For a $200,000 loan, the difference is about $6,228 for that 0.5% difference in the rate. So negotiating a rate downward by a half percentage point makes a difference, and the larger the loan is, the more the dollar value of the savings.

   The interest rate can also be either fixed or adjustable. Although these terms are most often associated with residential mortgage loans, they can also be applied to business loans of many types and have varying terms. An interest-only loan can be renegotiable after a few years. However, the rate you will be expected to pay is likely to change based on the interest market at the time. In this respect, the interest rate—unless fixed for the full term of the loan—is the great variable in the evaluation.

4. Compounding Method

The previous cases have all been based on monthly compounding of interest. In other words, the *nominal rate* (the annual rate stated by the lender) is divided by 12 (months), and the resulting monthly interest is calculated against the current loan balance. This method results in an annual rate higher than the nominal rate. As you might expect, the higher your interest rate, the more expensive monthly compounding is going to be.

Banks may charge monthly compounding rates for the money they loan, while paying you only quarterly compounded interest for funds you leave on deposit. Though this is not equitable, the banks also know that *you* need the loan at least as much as they want to grant it. Most managers pay little attention to the compounding method because it does not make much difference in the actual rate. For example, 7.5% compounded monthly comes out to an annual rate of 7.76% (compounding is explained later in this chapter). In comparison, quarterly compounding produces an annual rate of 7.71%, or only 0.005% less. The difference over the loan's repayment term adds up.

Simple Interest. To calculate interest, whether on a loan or a savings account, the basic formula—simple interest—is easy. Just multiply the stated interest rate by the principal amount (the amount borrowed).

Simple interest

$P \times R = I$

where: P = principal
R = interest rate
I = interest

On a spreadsheet, enter the following:

A1   P
B1   R
C1   = SUM(A1*B1)

► Example: The amount you are thinking about borrowing for a short-term working capital loan is $5,000. The rate you are quoted is 8.0%. Simple interest is calculated as:

$5,000 \times 8.0\% = \$400$

The spreadsheet values are:

A1   5,000
B1   0.08

BASIC MATH REVIEW

When multiplying by a percentage, convert the stated rate to decimal form. Shift the decimal two places to the left or divide by 100; either method produces the same result.

Percentage Conversion to Decimal: Decimal Shift

$r.0\% = 00r.0 = 0.0r$

Percentage Conversion to Decimal: Divide by 100

$r \div 100 = D$

where: r = percentage rate
        D = decimal equivalent

▶ **Example: At 8.0%:**

$8.0\% \div 100 = 0.08$

The recalculated decimal equivalent is used as the multiplier in the simple interest calculation. To make this calculation on a spreadsheet program, enter the following values:

A1   R
B1   = SUM(A1/100)

Based on the preceding example, A1 is the value 8.00, and this results in a shift to C1 of 0.08.

Simple interest may be used for calculations in some loans, especially those due in one year or less. However, it is rarely used for most business loans. This calculation works as a sensible starting point for more complex interest calculations and for making comparisons between the stated, or nominal, rate and the annual compound rate.

Daily Compound Interest. Most interest is compounded more than once per year. The most common rates are monthly and quarterly. The *periodic rate* of interest (the rate paid per partial-year period based on compounding method) is the rate per cycle of compounding. For example, monthly compounding is equal to one-twelfth of the stated annual rate, which is each month's periodic rate. Quarterly compounding has a periodic rate of one-quarter (of the year). So there are 12 periods for monthly compounding and four for quarterly compounding. To find the periodic rate, divide the stated rate by the number of periods in the year.

Periodic Rate

$$R \div p = i$$

where: R = nominal interest rate
         p = number of periods
         i = periodic interest rate

On a spreadsheet program, enter the following values:

A1   R
B   1P
C1   = SUM(A1/B1)

▶ Example: Your stated interest rate is 7.5%. Compounding takes place monthly, meaning there are 12 periods in the year. The periodic rate in this case is:

7.5% ÷ 12 = 0.625%, or 0.00625 decimal

Spreadsheet values are:

A1   7.5
B1   12

Recall the conversion formula. To convert 7.5% to decimal form, shift the decimal two places to the left or divide by 100:

7.5 ÷ 100 = 0.075 decimal

Next, the decimal equivalent is divided by the number of periods. For monthly compounding, divide by 12:

0.075 ÷ 12 = 0.00625%

You need to know the periodic rate to calculate interest for each period and to figure out the compound annual rate. The method requiring the greatest amount of calculation, daily compounding, has a periodic rate of either 360 or 365. Using 365 is called the *full-year method*, and using 360 is known as the *banker's year method*.

To calculate daily compounding (using the 365-day method), first divide the full year's interest rate by 365. This produces the daily periodic rate.

Daily Periodic Rate (365 Days)

$R \div 365 = i$

where: R = stated annual interest rate
i = periodic interest rate (365 days)

On a spreadsheet program, enter:

A1   R (IN DECIMAL FORM)
B1   = SUM(A1/B1)

▶ Example: Your stated interest rate is 7.5% (or a decimal equivalent of 0.075). The method used for calculating interest is daily, based on the 365-days-per-year rate. The daily period rate is:

0.075 ÷ 365 = 0.0002055

Once you compute the daily rate, each day's interest is computed with a series of steps:

1. Add 1 to the daily rate. This is the first day's multiplier for a debt:
   0.0002055 + 1 = 1.0002055
2. Multiply the sum in the previous step by the amount of the debt. For

example, if the amount borrowed is $8,000, the first day's debt (principal plus interest) interest is:

1.0002055 × $8,000.00 = $8,001.64

3. To calculate subsequent days of the accumulated debt, multiply the preceding answer by the initial daily rate in step 1:

1.0002055 × $8,001.64 = 8,003.28

To calculate the effective interest for several days, you can use a shortcut method. Multiply the daily rate by the number of additional days and then by the initial sum.

▶ Example: If you want to calculate the interest as of the fifth day, multiply the daily rate by itself four times (for days two through five) and then by the principal amount:

1.0002055 × 0.0002055 × 1.0002055 × 1.0002055 × 1.0002055 × $8,000.00 = $8,008.22

A shorthand version of this formula is:

1.0002055^5 × $8,000.00 = $8,008.22

This can be verified by checking the steps for each of the five days:

Day	Rate	Total
		$8,000.00
1	1.0002055	8,001.64
2	1.0002055	8,003.29
3	1.0002055	8,004.93
4	1.0002055	8,006.58
5	1.0002055	8,008.22

The formula for calculating daily compounding is:

Daily Compounding

$[1 + (R \div i)^n] \times P = C$

where: R = stated annual interest rate
i = periodic interest rate (365 days)

n = number of periods to be compounded
P = principal
C = compounded value

This series of calculations can also be placed on a worksheet and calculated using the formula feature. For spreadsheet programs, the following formulas are needed based on the placement of information in named cells:

DAILY COMPOUNDING

A1	ANNUAL INTEREST RATE DIVIDED BY 365	
	= DAILY RATE, PLUS 1	= SUM(I/365) + 1
B1	PRINCIPAL AMOUNT	
C1	ACCUMULATED AMOUNT	= SUM(A1*B1)
A2		= A1
B2		= C1
	COPY C1	
	PASTE TO C2	
	COPY A2, B2, AND C2	
	PASTE TO ROW 3, COLUMNS 1, 2, AND 3	
	REPEAT PASTE FOR EACH ROW	

This process is carried forward to as many days as you need. A fast shortcut for finding the effective daily rate for a large number of days is to multiply the daily rate (A3) by itself for as many days as needed (remembering that the initial sum is the first day).

▶ Example: For the rate applicable on the 20th day, multiply the rate 19 more times by itself. You can do this on any calculator by entering the amount, then the multiplication (×) button, and then the equals (=) button 19 times. In the case of the 7.5% annual (compounded daily), the 20th day's rate is:

$1.0002055^{20} = 1.0041180$

Next, multiply this by $8,000.00:

$1.0041180 \times \$8,000.00 = \$8,032.94$

The outcome for 20 days based on the spreadsheet formula is summarized in Table 1-1.

The formula for calculating the daily debt (principal plus interest) is also called the *accumulated value of 1*. A visual representation of the concept of compounding interest on a single deposit is shown in Figure 1-1.

Annual, Semiannual, and Quarterly Interest. The calculations for daily interest are far more complex than for annual (once-per-year), semiannual (twice-per-year), and quarterly (four-times-per-year) compounding.

Annual interest is not the same as simple interest, which involves no compounding. In the case of annual interest, compounding takes place

TABLE 1-1 DAILY COMPOUNDING (365-DAY RATE)

Deposit amount = $8,000.00
Interest rate = 7.5%
Term: 20 days

Day	A	B	C (Value)
1	1.000205479	8,000.00	8001.64
2	1.000205479	8001.644	8003.29
3	1.000205479	8003.288	8004.93
4	1.000205479	8004.933	8006.58
5	1.000205479	8006.577	8008.22
6	1.000205479	8008.223	8009.87
7	1.000205479	8009.868	8011.51
8	1.000205479	8011.514	8013.16
9	1.000205479	8013.16	8014.81
10	1.000205479	8014.807	8016.45
11	1.000205479	8016.454	8018.10
12	1.000205479	8018.101	8019.75
13	1.000205479	8019.748	8021.40
14	1.000205479	8021.396	8023.04
15	1.000205479	8023.044	8024.69
16	1.000205479	8024.693	8026.34
17	1.000205479	8026.342	8027.99
18	1.000205479	8027.991	8029.64
19	1.000205479	8029.641	8031.29
20	1.000205479	8031.291	8032.94

FIGURE 1-1 ACCUMULATED VALUE OF A SINGLE DEPOSIT

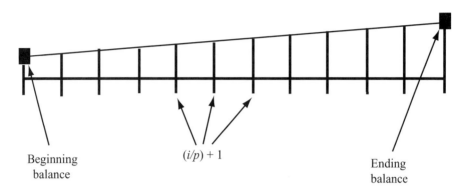

Beginning balance

$(i/p) + 1$

Ending balance

only once per year. So over three years, the rate grows because interest is earned on interest, even though the calculation is only done annually. Simple interest involves no compounding at all. Annual compounding is an unusual calculation and is likely to be found only in private loans, such as loans between a business and a family member. To calculate annual interest, compound the stated annual interest every year.

▶ Example: An $8,000 loan at 7.5% with annual compounding involves a three-year calculation of a straight 8% at the end of each year:

Year	Interest	Total
		$8,000.00
1	$ 600.00	8,600.00
2	645.00	9,245.00
3	693.38	9,938.38

The calculation for annual compounding to arrive at the total debt is:

Annual Compounding

$(i + 1)^x \times P = D$

where: i = annual interest rate

x = number of years

P = principal deposited

D = total debt as of the number of years

▶ Example: Applying this formula to the example, the formula is:

$(0.075\% + 1)^3 \times \$8,000.00 = \$9,938.38$

This can be summarized on a spreadsheet, with the following fields and values. (Note that the first calculation is the combined decimal equivalent of the interest rate plus 1; so 7.5% is equal to 0.075 + 1, or 1.075.)

ANNUAL COMPOUNDING

A1	ANNUAL INTEREST RATE PLUS 1	$= \text{SUM}(\text{I} + 1)$
B1	PRINCIPAL AMOUNT	
C1	ACCUMULATED AMOUNT	$= \text{SUM}(A1*B1)$
A2		$= A1$
B2		$= C1$

COPY C1
PASTE TO C2
COPY A2, B2, AND C2
PASTE TO ROW 3, COLUMNS 1, 2, AND 3
REPEAT PASTE FOR EACH ROW

The outcome for three years using the spreadsheet program is shown in Table 1-2.

TABLE 1-2 ANNUAL COMPOUNDING

Deposit amount = $8,000.00
Interest rate = 7.5%
Term: 3 years

Year	A	B	C (Value)
1	1.075	8,000	8600.00
2	1.075	8600	9245.00
3	1.075	9245	9938.38

Semiannual interest is calculated twice per year.

▶ Example: Using the same example, a three-year term requires six calculations rather than three, based on a periodic rate equal to one-half of the annual rate. Since the annual rate is 7.5% (decimal equivalent 0.075), the semiannual periodic rate is:

$$0.075 \div 2 = 0.0375$$

BASIC MATH REVIEW

An easy conversion from percentage to decimal is to shift the decimal point two places to the left.

The three-year accumulation of interest and principal in the case of semiannual compounding is:

Period	Interest	Total
		$8,000.00
1	$ 300.00	8,300.00
2	311.25	8,611.25
3	322.92	8,934.17
4	335.03	9,269.20
5	347.60	9,616.80
6	360.63	9,977.43

This method produces an additional $39.05 above annual compounding.

The more often the compounding is performed, the higher the compounding effect. The formula for semiannual compounding is:

Semiannual compounding

$$[(i \div 2) + 1]^x \times P = D$$

where: i = annual interest rate
x = number of semiannual periods
P = principal deposited
D = total debt as of the number of periods

▶ Example: Applying this formula to the example, an $8,000 deposit with 7.5% semiannual interest for six periods (three years) results in a sum of:

[(0.075 ÷ 2) + 1⁶] × \$8,000.00 = \$9,977.43

This can be summarized on a spreadsheet, with the following fields and values. (Note that the first calculation is the combined decimal equivalent of the interest rate plus 1; so the half-year rate of 3.75% is equal to 0.0375 + 1, or 1.0375.)

SEMIANNUAL COMPOUNDING

A1	ANNUAL INTEREST RATE PLUS 1	= SUM(I/2) + 1
B1	PRINCIPAL AMOUNT	
C1	ACCUMULATED AMOUNT	= SUM(A1*B1)
A2		= A1
B2		= C1

COPY C1
PASTE TO C2
COPY A2, B2, AND C2
PASTE TO ROW 3, COLUMNS 1, 2, AND 3
REPEAT PASTE FOR EACH ROW

The calculations on the spreadsheet program are summarized for six periods in Table 1-3.

A more common calculation of interest is based on quarterly compounding, or a calculation of interest four times per year.

▶ Example: Over a three-year period, you would have 12 periods to calculate (3 years times 4 years). Based on \$8,000 at 7.5% compounded quarterly (1.875% per quarter):

TABLE 1-3 SEMIANNUAL COMPOUNDING

Deposit amount = \$8,000.00
Interest rate = 7.5%
Term: 3 years (6 semiannual periods)

Period	A	B	C (Value)
1	1.0375	8000.00	8300.00
2	1.0375	8300.00	8611.25
3	1.0375	8611.25	8934.17
4	1.0375	8934.17	9269.20
5	1.0375	9269.20	9616.80
6	1.0375	9616.80	9977.43

Period	Interest	Total
		$8,000.00
1	$ 150.00	8,150.00
2	152.81	8,302.81
3	155.68	8,458.49
4	158.60	8,617.09
5	161.57	8,778.66
6	164.60	8,943.26
7	167.68	9,110.94
8	170.83	9,281.77
9	174.03	9,455.80
10	177.30	9,633.10
11	180.62	9,813.72
12	184.01	9,997.73

Quarterly Compounding

$$[(\,i \div 4\,) + 1]^x \times P = D$$

where: i = annual interest rate
x = number of quarterly periods
P = principal deposited
D = total debt as of the number of periods

▶ Example: Based on the same $8,000.00 deposit but using 7.5% and quarterly compounding, the formula for a three-year accumulation is:

$$\{[(0.075 \div 4) + 1]^{12}\} \times \$8,000.00 = \$9,997.86$$

Quarterly compounding can be summarized on a spreadsheet, with the following fields and values. (Note that the first calculation is the combined decimal equivalent of the interest rate plus 1; so the quarterly rate of 1.875% is equal to 0.01875 + 1, or 1.01875.)

QUARTERLY COMPOUNDING

A1	ANNUAL INTEREST RATE PLUS 1	= SUM(I/4) + 1
B1	PRINCIPAL AMOUNT	
C1	ACCUMULATED AMOUNT	= SUM(A1*B1)
A2		= A1
B2		= C1

COPY C1

PASTE TO C2

COPY A2, B2, AND C2

PASTE TO ROW 3, COLUMNS 1, 2, AND 3

The formula based on this example as it appears on a spreadsheet is summarized in Table 1-4.

Monthly Compounding. The best-known and most widely used calculation is monthly compounding. This method is used on virtually all mortgages and commercial loans. It involves dividing the nominal rate by 12 (months) and then applying the periodic rate to each month's outstanding balance.

▶ Example: An $8,000 deposit at 7.5% compounded monthly involves 12 calculations per year, each at 1/12 the nominal rate, or 0.00625%:

$0.075 \div 12 = 0.00625$

Monthly Compounding

$$[(i \div 12) + 1]^x \times P = D$$

TABLE 1-4 *QUARTERLY COMPOUNDING*

Deposit amount = $8,000.00
Interest rate = 7.5%
Term: 3 years (12 quarterly periods)

Period	A	B	C (Value)
1	1.01875	8000.00	8150.00
2	1.01875	8150.00	8302.81
3	1.01875	8302.81	8458.49
4	1.01875	8458.49	8617.09
5	1.01875	8617.09	8778.66
6	1.01875	8778.66	8943.26
7	1.01875	8943.26	9110.94
8	1.01875	9110.94	9281.77
9	1.01875	9281.77	9455.81
10	1.01875	9455.81	9633.10
11	1.01875	9633.10	9813.72
12	1.01875	9813.72	9997.73

where: i = annual interest rate
　　　　x = number of months
　　　　P = principal deposited
　　　　D = total debt as of the number of months

Over a one-year period, the formula involves 12 calculations, with each month's interest at 0.00625. The first year's calculations are:

Month	Interest	Total
		$8,000.00
1	$ 50.00	8,050.00
2	50.31	8,100.31
3	50.63	8,150.94
4	50.94	8,201.88
5	51.26	8,253.14
6	51.58	8,304.73
7	51.90	8,356.63
8	52.23	8,408.86
9	52.56	8,461.42
10	52.88	8,514.30
11	53.21	8,567.51
12	53.55	8,621.06

▶ Example: Apply the formula summarizing this calculation:

$$[(0.075 \div 12) + 1]^{12} \times \$8,000.00 = \$8,621.05$$

This calculation can also be summarized on a spreadsheet with the same design as that shown for previous compounding methods. The annual rate, expressed in decimal form, is 0.075 and, when divided by 12, produces the monthly rate of 0.00625. When 1 is added, the monthly multiplier is the result:

$$(0.075 \div 12) + 1 = 1.00625 \text{ decimal}$$

Here is a summary of the spreadsheet programming for monthly compounding:

MONTHLY COMPOUNDING

A1	ANNUAL INTEREST RATE PLUS 1	$= SUM(I/12) + 1$
B1	PRINCIPAL AMOUNT	

C1	ACCUMULATED AMOUNT	$=$ SUM(A1*B1)
A2		$=$ A1
B2		$=$ C1
	COPY C1	
	PASTE TO C2	
	COPY A2, B2, AND C2	
	PASTE TO ROW 3, COLUMNS 1, 2, AND 3	

A summary of the spreadsheet rows and columns is provided in Table 1-5.

Although many free calculators are easily found online for these calculations, you'll find it useful to be aware of how the calculations are performed. This understanding improves your basic comprehension of the functions involved and provides you with the ability to make calculations even when online calculators are not available at the moment.

TABLE 1-5 MONTHLY COMPOUNDING

Deposit amount = $8,000.00
Interest rate = 7.5%
Term: 1 year (12 months)

Period	A	B	C (Value)
1	1.00625	8000.00	8050.00
2	1.00625	8050.00	8100.31
3	1.00625	8100.31	8150.94
4	1.00625	8150.94	8201.88
5	1.00625	8201.88	8253.14
6	1.00625	8253.14	8304.73
7	1.00625	8304.73	8356.63
8	1.00625	8356.63	8408.86
9	1.00625	8408.86	8461.42
10	1.00625	8461.42	8514.30
11	1.00625	8514.30	8567.51
12	1.00625	8567.5	18621.06

ACCUMULATED VALUE OF A SERIES OF DEPOSITS

Calculating the accumulated value of a single deposit over various compounding periods is far easier than calculating how a fund grows with a *series* of deposits over time. However, the latter calculation has widespread business applications. For example, if you are setting up a reserve with monthly deposits or putting funds aside for expansion, you need to calculate how monthly deposits will grow over a period of months or years.

This calculation is going to vary based on the compounding method used. The more frequently the compounding occurs, the more interest accumulates. However, the periodic interest rate used in the following calculations is going to vary; so keep this difference in mind.

▶ Example: A 7.5% annual nominal rate over three years entails different period rates and a different number of periods in the calculation:

Periodic Interest Rate (7.5% annual rate, three years):

Method	Periods	Periodic Rate
Monthly	36	0.00625
Quarterly	12	0.01875
Semiannually	6	0.0375
Annually	3	0.075

In this formula, you need to calculate the growing effect of a series of deposits over time, and that effect varies with the amount deposited, interest rate, overall time involved, and compounding method.

Accumulated Value of a Series of Deposits

$$D \{[(1 + R)^n - 1] \div R\} = A$$

where: D = periodic deposit amount
R = periodic interest rate
n = number of periods
A = accumulated value

The accumulated value of a series of deposits is further illustrated in Figure 1-2.

FIGURE 1-2 ACCUMULATED VALUE OF A SERIES OF DEPOSITS

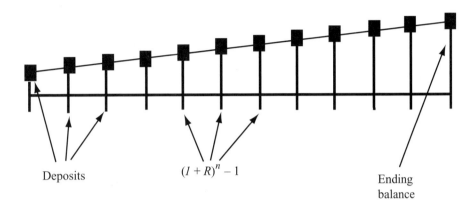

Deposits $(1 + R)^n - 1$ Ending
                                                              balance

▶ Example: You are putting aside $300 per month for three years. Your
fund is estimated to yield 7.5% compounded monthly. The formula is:

$300.00\{[(1 + 0.00625)^{36} - 1] \div 0.00625\}$ = Accumulated value
$300.00 [(1.251446 - 1] \div 0.00625\}$ = Accumulated value
$300.00 (40.23136) = $12,069.41

This formula can also be calculated using a spreadsheet formula program:

ACCUMULATED VALUE OF A SERIES OF DEPOSITS

A1	PERIODIC DEPOSIT AMOUNT	
B1	PERIODIC INTEREST RATE + 1	= SUM(1 + R)
C1		= B1
B2		= B1
C2		= SUM(C1 * B2)
	COPY B AND C, ROW 3	
	PASTE TO SUBSEQUENT B AND C ROWS	
D36	(ASSUMING 36 PERIODS TOTAL)	= SUM(C36-1)/(C1-1)
E36		= SUM(D36*A1)

The outcome of the spreadsheet columns and rows is summarized in
Table 1-6.

TABLE 1-6 ACCUMULATED VALUE OF A SERIES OF DEPOSITS

Deposit amount = $300 per month
Interest rate = 7.5% compounded monthly
Term: 3 years (36 months)

Period	A	B	C	D	E (Final Value)
1	300	1.00625	1.00625		
2		1.00625	1.012539063		
3		1.00625	1.018867432		
4		1.00625	1.025235353		
5		1.00625	1.031643074		
6		1.00625	1.038090843		
12		1.00625	1.077632599		
18		1.00625	1.118680533		
24		1.00625	1.161292018		
30		1.00625	1.20552661		
36		1.00625	1.251446136	40.2313817	12069.41

The various methods of calculating return can be not only greatly simplified by using a few formulas, but especially effective when they are programmed into a spreadsheet. Once your spreadsheet is set up to make the calculations, you can deal with the variables in a budget or forecast with great flexibility. For each set of variables, enter the annual interest rate and compounding method into the formula, and let the spreadsheet do the work, ensuring not only ease but also the accuracy of calculations, even for extended time periods.

In setting up the spreadsheet program, copied fields can be pasted into multiple other fields all at once rather than one at a time. For example, in calculating daily compounding, once your formula has been entered into the first cell, you can extend the daily outcome to all 365 fields in a single step. This is the kind of feature that makes spreadsheet formulas effective and easy to use.

LOOKING AHEAD

The next chapter introduces more advanced calculations, including present and future value. Although these formulas are more complex than calculating interest on single or periodic deposits, they too can be simplified and managed by programming formulas onto a spreadsheet.

C H A P T E R   2

Present Value and Sinking Funds

This chapter tackles more complex formulas than those of the previous chapter and answers a different but equally important set of questions. The accumulation of interest on a single deposit answers the question, "How much will a single sum grow over a specified period of time, given a known rate of interest and compounding method?" The accumulation of a series of deposits answers a variation of that question: "How much will a series of deposits grow over time, based on a known rate of interest and compounding method?"

This chapter deals with two concepts:

- *Present value:* How much you need to deposit today to have what you need at some point in the future.

- *Sinking fund payments:* How much you need to deposit over time to have what you need at some point in the future.

Both concepts are based on knowing the desired end result and on determining how much you need to deposit today to achieve that balance. For managers, present value calculations are likely to be more pressing than tracking savings accounts. For example, if a business needs to set aside a reserve for future losses, save money to purchase equipment, or better manage cash flow by setting up a series of payments, present value calculations are going to be a part of the required exercise.

PRESENT VALUE OF A SINGLE DEPOSIT

That money accumulates based on combinations of principal and interest is a fairly well understood concept, even if the calculations are not. On the other side of the compounding interest calculation is present value. This value is needed to identify how much to save for a target number in the future with either a single deposit or a series of deposits or how to pay off a loan within a number of months or years.

The first of these calculations is called the *present value of a single deposit*. It answers the question, "How much money do I need to deposit today, given a known rate of interest, compounding method, and time period, to accumulate a target amount in the future?"

▶ Example: You plan to purchase a new piece of machinery in five years at an estimated cost of $8,000. You do not want to finance this purchase but prefer to save up for it. So you need to know how much money you need to put away now to have $8,000 in five years. You have identified a very successful mutual fund that has averaged a 7.5% return for the past three years. Based on the assumption that this rate continues for the next five years, you need to know how much to put aside right now.

A calculation like this is always based on a series of assumptions. Among these is the most obvious one: that the mutual fund will achieve the same average rate of return in the future as it has in the past. Second is the assumption that you will reinvest all earnings (dividends, interest, and capital gains) because, to accomplish your goal, you need the compounded rate of return. You also need to determine which compounding method is best to use. The advantage of formatting a calculation in a spreadsheet is that all of the variables can be changed, and all the outcomes will change accordingly and automatically. Even if you have entered monthly outcomes for five years (60 months), as soon as the variables change, you can also change the variables to keep the exercise realistic. If your mutual fund loses money in the first three months, your net fund will be worth less. By depositing additional funds (changing the variable), you can create a revised worksheet. If the fund's performance is unexpectedly positive, you can instantly see how much excess your five-year plan will create; the excess can be treated as a type of reserve against future cyclical downturns.

To calculate the present value of a single deposit, you need only to know what assumptions you will use: the annual average earnings rate, compounding method, and desired end-result fund. Here is the formula:

Present Value of a Single Deposit

$$\{1 \div [1 + (i \div p)]^n\} \times D = V$$

where: i = annual interest rate
p = number of periods in the compounding method
n = periods until the deposit amount is needed
D = end-result deposit
V = amount needed to be deposited today

This formula is not actually as complex as it looks at first glance. The value 1 is divided by a series of familiar calculations. The annual interest rate has to be reduced to the periodic rate, and then the number of periods (normally months) is calculated. A visual look at this is shown in Figure 2-1.

For monthly compounding, the annual rate has to be divided by a p of 12; for quarterly, p is 4. The resulting factor (which will be a decimal value less than 1) is then multiplied by the amount of deposit needed at the end of the period in order to find the value of the single deposit you need today.

▶ Example: You want to accumulate a fund of $8,000 in five years. Your assumed rate on an investment in a mutual fund is 7.5%, and you will calculate compounding monthly. How much do you need to place on deposit today? Apply the formula. This can be reflected in

FIGURE 2-1 PRESENT VALUE OF A SINGLE DEPOSIT

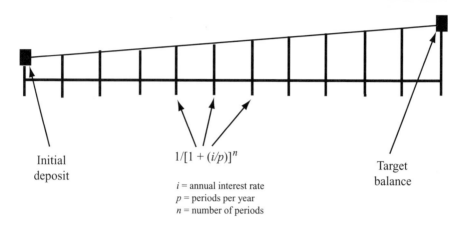

Initial deposit

$1/[1 + (i/p)]^{n}$

i = annual interest rate
p = periods per year
n = number of periods

Target balance

a spreadsheet and then manipulated to check outcomes with varying assumptions.

Here is the spreadsheet formula:

PRESENT VALUE OF A SINGLE DEPOSIT

A1	PERIODIC INTEREST RATE PLUS 1	$=$ SUM(1 $+$ (I/P))
B1		$=$ A1
A2		$=$ A1
B2		$=$ SUM(A2*B1)
	COPY ROW 2, COLUMNS A AND B	
	PASTE TO SUBSEQUENT ROWS	
C60	(ASSUMING 60 MONTHS TOTAL)	$=$ SUM(1/B60)
D60	DEPOSIT NEEDED TODAY	$=$ SUM(C60*D)

This formula presents a scenario based on well-understood assumptions. However, if you need to alter your assumptions, a copy-and-paste operation is easy to perform.

▶ Example, if you decide you need to meet your $8,000 target in 52 months instead of 60 months, you can copy cell C60 and D60 and paste them into cells C52 and D52. The result is $5,786.07, the amount you need to deposit today rather than the 60-month outcome of $5,504.73.

The outcome of this calculation is summarized in Table 2-1.

SINKING FUND PAYMENTS AND PRESENT VALUE PER PERIOD

Sinking Fund Payments

Making a single deposit at the beginning of a period is rarely a practical idea. Managers are likely to make a series of monthly deposits into a sinking fund over a period of months to accumulate a known future

TABLE 2-1 PRESENT VALUE OF A SINGLE DEPOSIT

Final deposit amount = $8,000.00
Interest rate = 7.5%
Term: 60 months

Month	A	B	C	D
1	1.00625	1.00625		
2	1.00625	1.01254		
3	1.00625	1.01887		
4	1.00625	1.02524		
5	1.00625	1.03164		
6	1.00625	1.03809		
7	1.00625	1.04458		
8	1.00625	1.05111		
9	1.00625	1.05768		
10	1.00625	1.06429		
15	1.00625	1.09796		
20	1.00625	1.13271		
25	1.00625	1.16855		
30	1.00625	1.20553		
35	1.00625	1.24367		
40	1.00625	1.28303		
45	1.00625	1.32363		
50	1.00625	1.36551		
55	1.00625	1.40872		
60	1.00625	1.45329	0.688091824	5504.73

value. The sinking fund payment is a calculation of a series based on known assumptions. It answers the question, "How much money do I need to deposit per month, given a known rate of interest, compounding method, and time period, to accumulate a target amount in the future?"

As you would expect, the formula for this calculation is more complex than for a single deposit. It involves figuring out compound interest over many months and based on a series of payments into a fund. Here is the formula for sinking fund payments:

Sinking Fund Payments

$$D \times (i \div p) \div \{[1 + (i \div p)]^n - 1\}) = V$$

where: D = target deposit
i = annual interest rate
p = number of periods in the compounding method
n = periods until the deposit amount is needed
V = amount of periodic deposits required

This formula is complex because it requires a double level of division functions. However, it is simplified when placed in a spreadsheet program. In addition, it is better comprehended when viewed; refer to Figure 2-2 for a visual summary of this formula.

Example: You want to accumulate $8,000 in 60 months. Your assumptions are that you will earn 7.5% per month, compounded

FIGURE 2-2 SINKING FUND PAYMENTS

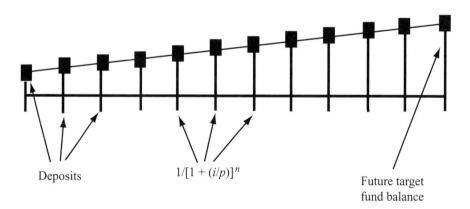

Deposits $1/[1 + (i/p)]^n$

Future target
fund balance

monthly (12 times per year). You need to know the value of a series of deposits (sinking fund payments) required for the next 60 months based on these assumptions.

SINKING FUND PAYMENTS

A1	PERIODIC INTEREST RATE PLUS 1	$= SUM(1 + (I/P))$
B1		$= A1$
A2		$= A1$
B2		$= SUM(A2*B1)$
	COPY ROW 2, COLUMNS A AND B	
	PASTE TO SUBSEQUENT ROWS	
C60		$= SUM(A1-1)/(B60-1)$
D60	DEPOSITS NEEDED	$= SUM(C60*D)$

In the example, the values of these abbreviations are:

where: i = 0.075 (7.5% in decimal form)
p = 12 (periods required for monthly compounding)
D = $8,000 (the fund needed at the end of 60 months)

The required monthly deposit is $110.30 for 60 months to create a fund worth $8,000.00.

Present Value per Period

In calculating the present value per period, you are answering the question, "How much do I need to deposit today to make a series of withdrawals over a specific period of time, assuming a rate of interest, compounding method, and number of months?"

The amount needed today to fall to zero at the end of the period, based on the amount of each withdrawal, the number of months, interest rate, and compounding method.

▶ Example: You want to set up a reserve and draw $300 against it each month for five years.

This kind of calculation occurs when you are going through a business expansion or retiring obligations based on fixed monthly payments. The formula for the present value per period is:

Present Value per Period

$$W \times \{1 \div [1 + (i \div p)^n]\} \div (i \div p) = D$$

where: W = periodic withdrawal amounts
$\quad\quad\;\; i$ = annual interest rate
$\quad\quad\; p$ = number of periods in the compounding method
$\quad\quad\; n$ = periods until the deposit amount is depleted
$\quad\quad\; D$ = initial deposit required

This formula produces the dollar amount needed to be deposited at the beginning of the term, based on monthly withdrawals, interest rate, compounding method, and number of months.

▶ Example: The desired withdrawal amount in the preceding example was $300 per month for five years (60 months), based on monthly compounding of a 7.5% annual rate. The outcome can be placed on a spreadsheet:

PRESENT VALUE PER PERIOD

A1	PERIODIC INTEREST RATE PLUS 1	=SUM(1 + (I/P))
B1		=A1
A2		=A1
B2		=SUM(A2*B1)
	COPY ROW 2, COLUMNS A AND B	
	PASTE TO SUBSEQUENT ROWS	
C60		=SUM(1-(1/B60))
D60	DOLLAR AMOUNT TO BE DEPOSITED	=SUM(C60/(A1-1))*W

The variables are:

$\quad i$ = 0.075 (decimal equivalent of 7.5%)
$\quad p$ = 12 (periods in monthly compounding)
$\quad W$ = $300 monthly withdrawal amount

Based on this calculation, you need to deposit $14,971.59 to withdraw $300 per month for 60 months and deplete the fund. The calculation is summarized, based on the spreadsheet, in Table 2-2. The present

TABLE 2-2 PRESENT VALUE PER PERIOD

Monthly withdrawal amount = $300
Interest rate = 7.5%
Term: 60 months

Month	A	B	C	D
1	1.00625	1.00625		
2	1.00625	1.01254		
3	1.00625	1.01887		
4	1.00625	1.02524		
5	1.00625	1.03164		
6	1.00625	1.03809		
7	1.00625	1.04458		
8	1.00625	1.05111		
9	1.00625	1.05768		
10	1.00625	1.06429		
15	1.00625	1.09796		
20	1.00625	1.13271		
25	1.00625	1.16855		
30	1.00625	1.20553		
35	1.00625	1.24367		
40	1.00625	1.28303		
45	1.00625	1.32363		
50	1.00625	1.36551		
55	1.00625	1.40872		
60	1.00625	1.45329	0.311908176	14,971.59

value per period time line is shown in Figure 2-3. The calculated spreadsheet results are summarized in Table 2-3.

LOAN AMORTIZATION

Yet another variety of the present value formula is loan amortization. This is the procedure used to retire any long-term debt and is best-known for mortgages. Loan terms require you to amortize (pay down) the loan each month. Every payment consists of principal and interest, with the interest calculated based on the outstanding balance. For this reason, interest is high during the early years of a repayment schedule and declines over time.

FIGURE 2-3 PRESENT VALUE PER PERIOD

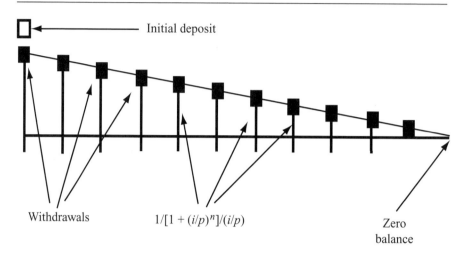

▶ Example: You purchase the building where your company is based and make payments over a period of years. You take a 30-year mortgage at 7.5%, and it takes 22 out of 30 years to pay off one-half of the debt, with the remaining 50% paid during the last eight years.

The reasons for the slow decline in mortgage principal all have to do with interest. To calculate loan amortization, the formula incorporates the formula for the present value per period in a more involved calculation. The present value per period introduced in the preceding section was:

$$W \times \{1 \div [1 + (i \div p)^n]\} \div (i \div p) = D$$

where: W = periodic withdrawal amounts
      i = annual interest rate
      p = number of periods in the compounding method
      n = periods until the deposit amount is depleted
      D = initial deposit required

This is slightly modified as part of the loan amortization formula. The loan amortization formula results in the required monthly pay-

TABLE 2-3 SINKING FUND PAYMENTS

Final deposit amount = $8,000.00
Interest rate = 7.5%
Term: 60 months

Month	A	B	C	D
1	1.00625	1.00625		
2	1.00625	1.01254		
3	1.00625	1.01887		
4	1.00625	1.02524		
5	1.00625	1.03164		
6	1.00625	1.03809		
7	1.00625	1.04458		
8	1.00625	1.05111		
9	1.00625	1.05768		
10	1.00625	1.06429		
15	1.00625	1.09796		
20	1.00625	1.13271		
25	1.00625	1.16855		
30	1.00625	1.20553		
35	1.00625	1.24367		
40	1.00625	1.28303		
45	1.00625	1.32363		
50	1.00625	1.36551		
55	1.00625	1.40872		
60	1.00625	1.45329	0.013787949	110.30

ment to retire the full loan balance. So the present value of 1 per period formula is:

$$\{1 \div [1 + (i \div p)^n]\} \div (i \div p)$$

Loan Amortization (Summarized)

$$L \times [(R \times (P^n)] \div [(P^n) \times 1)] = A$$

where: L = original balance of the loan
R = periodic interest rate (annual rate divided by periods per year)
P = present value of 1
n = number of periods (usually months)
A = required payment per period

This formula and its outcome are summarized in Figure 2-4.

This formula can also be summarized on a spreadsheet program using the following equations:

LOAN AMORTIZATION

A1	PERIODIC INTEREST RATE PLUS 1	$= SUM(1 + (I/P))$
B1		$= A1$
A2		$= A1$
B2		$= SUM(A2*B1)$
	COPY ROW 2, COLUMNS A AND B	
	PASTE TO SUBSEQUENT ROWS	
C360	(ASSUMING A 30-YEAR MORTGAGE TERM, OR A TOTAL OF 360 MONTHS)	$= SUM(A360-1)*B360$
D360	PAYMENT REQUIRED	$+ SUM((C360/(B360-1))*L$

▶ Example: The outcome for 360 months, based on 7.5% compounded monthly and for a $10,000 loan, is a required payment of $69.92 per month. For example, if you contracted a $10,000 30-year mortgage on your home to generate working capital, your payments would be $69.92 per month.

Although this is a relatively small amount for a 30-year loan, a larger amount can be calculated easily by changing the spreadsheet variables. The calculations are summarized in Table 2-4.

FIGURE 2-4 LOAN AMORTIZATION

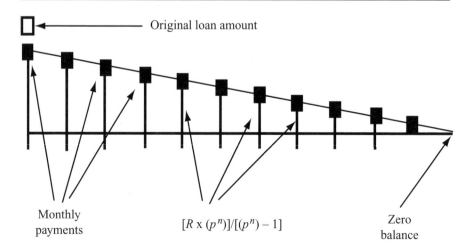

Original loan amount

Monthly payments

$[R \times (p^n)]/[(p^n) - 1]$

Zero balance

TABLE 2-4 LOAN AMORTIZATION

Amount borrowed = $10,000
Interest rate = 7.5%
Term: 360 months

Month	A	B	C	D
1	1.00625	1.006250		
2	1.00625	1.01254		
3	1.00625	1.01887		
4	1.00625	1.02524		
5	1.00625	1.03164		
10	1.00625	1.06429		
20	1.00625	1.13271		
40	1.00625	1.28303		
60	1.00625	1.45329		
80	1.00625	1.64616		
100	1.00625	1.86462		
120	1.00625	2.11206		
140	1.00625	2.39235		
160	1.00625	2.70984		
180	1.00625	3.06945		
200	1.00625	3.47679		
220	1.00625	3.93819		
240	1.00625	4.46082		
260	1.00625	5.0528		
280	1.00625	5.72335		
300	1.00625	6.48288		
320	1.00625	7.34321		
340	1.00625	8.31771		
360	1.00625	9.42153	0.058884587	69.92

Loan amortization payments can also be found in interest tables and online, including free online calculators.

When you are making payments on a loan, you also need to track several features to determine the status of the loan (and to ensure that the lender is making calculations accurately):

- The balance forward
- The amount assigned to interest and principal
- The percentage remaining on the loan

Four separate calculations are needed, and they can be reduced to a single spreadsheet program. The four calculations produce:

- Each month's interest
- Each month's principal
- A new balance forward
- The percentage of remaining balance on the loan

The four formulas are:

Monthly Interest on a Loan

$I = B \times (i \div p)$

where: I = monthly interest
B balance forward
i = annual interest rate
p = number of periods in the year (usually 12 months)

On a spreadsheet program:

```
A1    B
B1      = SUM(I/P)
C1      = SUM(A1*B1)
```

Monthly Principal on a Loan

$P = M - I$

where: P = monthly principal
M = monthly payment
I = monthly interest

On a spreadsheet program:

```
A1    M
B1    I
C1      = SUM(A1-B1)
```

New Balance Forward on a Loan

$N = B - P$

where: N = new monthly balance forward

$$B = \text{balance forward}$$
$$P = \text{monthly principal}$$

On a spreadsheet program:

```
A1    B
B1    P
C1      = SUM(A1-B1
```

Remaining Balance Percentage on a Loan

$$R = N \div L$$

where: R = remaining balance percentage
N = new monthly balance forward
L = original loan amount

On a spreadsheet program:

```
A1    N
B1    L
C1      = SUM(A1/B1)
```

These four steps are easily understood when their purpose and outcomes are summarized:

1. *Monthly Interest on a Loan.* The periodic rate (1/12th of the annual rate) is applied against the balance forward to calculate the current month's interest.
2. *Monthly Principal on a Loan.* The total monthly payment is reduced by the amount of interest to isolate the amount going to pay down the loan.
3. *New Balance Forward on a Loan.* The balance forward is reduced by the portion of the current month's payment going to principal.
4. *Remaining Balance Percentage on a Loan.* This is the percentage of the original loan remaining due after applying the current month's principal.

All these steps can be placed on a spreadsheet formula to produce a worksheet for the entire loan period or for a portion of it. The formulas are:

LOAN PAYMENTS AND BALANCES

A1	BALANCE FORWARD ($10,000 IN THE EXAMPLE USED)	B
B1	MONTHLY INTEREST (7.5% PER YEAR, COMPOUNDED MONTHLY)	$= SUM(A1*(I/P))$
C1	MONTHLY PRINCIPAL ($69.22 FOR 30 YEARS IN THE EXAMPLE)	$= SUM(M-B1)$
D1	NEW BALANCE FORWARD (PREVIOUS LESS PRINCIPAL)	$= SUM(A1-C1)$
E1	REMAINING BALANCE PERCENTAGE	$= SUM(D1/L)$
A1		$= D1$
	COPY B1, C1, D1, E1	
	PASTE TO B2, C2, D2, E2	
	COPY COLUMNS A THROUGH E, ROW 2	
	PASTE TO ALL SUBSEQUENT CELLS	

The formulas and outcome are summarized in Table 2-5.

READING LOAN AMORTIZATION TABLES

Rather than calculating the required monthly payment for every instance, you can use one of many free online calculators or look up loan amortization tables. These provide you with the interest rate, repayment term in years, the amount borrowed, and the required monthly payment. A typical summarized loan amortization schedule is shown in Figure 2-5.

You can also estimate the amount of a required payment within pennies for loan amounts not shown on a table.

▶ Example: The monthly payment over 30 years for borrowing $500 is $3.50 per month at 7.5%, as the table in Figure 2-5 reveals. For a loan of $1,000, the monthly payment is twice as much, or $7.00 per month. From this you can deduce that a loan halfway between the two

TABLE 2-5 LOAN PAYMENTS AND BALANCES

Amount borrowed = $10,000
Interest rate = 7.5%
Term: 360 months

Month	Balance Forward A	Interest B	Principal C	New Balance Forward D	Remaining Balance E
1	$10000.00	62.50	7.43	9992.57	99.93
2	9992.57	62.45	7.48	9985.09	99.85
3	9985.09	62.41	7.52	9977.57	99.78
4	9977.57	62.36	7.57	9970.00	99.70
5	9970.00	62.31	7.62	9962.38	99.62
6	9962.38	62.26	7.67	9954.72	99.55
7	9954.72	62.22	7.71	9947.00	99.47
8	9947.00	62.17	7.76	9939.24	99.39
9	9939.24	62.12	7.81	9931.43	99.31
10	9931.43	62.07	7.86	9923.58	99.24
40	9673.01	60.46	9.47	9663.54	96.64
80	9244.00	57.78	12.15	9231.85	92.32
120	8693.57	54.33	15.60	8677.98	86.78
160	7987.36	49.92	20.01	7967.35	79.67
200	7081.26	44.26	25.67	7055.59	70.56
240	5918.72	36.99	32.94	5885.78	58.86
280	4427.14	27.67	42.26	4384.88	43.85
320	2513.41	15.71	54.22	2459.19	24.59
360	58.05	0.36	58.05	0.00	0.00

loan amounts, $750, will require a payment that is the average of these two:

($3.50 + $7.00) ÷ 2 = $5.25

This can be further tested by reducing the required payment for a $75,000 loan by 1/100th. The table shows that a $75,000 loan requires a monthly payment of $524.42. Here are the calculations:

Amount borrowed: $75,000 ÷ 100 = $750
Monthly payment: $524.42 ÷ 100 = $5.24

Another way you can use tables for estimates is to calculate payments for interest rates not shown on the tables. If tables are reported in, say,

FIGURE 2-5 LOAN AMORTIZATION TABLE

TERM	5 YRS	10 YRS	15 YRS	20 YRS	25 YRS	30 YRS
7.5% Interest rate — Years to repay						
AMOUNT						
500	10.02	5.94	4.64	4.03	3.70	3.50
1,000	20.04	11.88	9.28	8.06	7.39	7.00
2,000	40.08	23.75	18.55	16.12	14.78	13.99
3,000	60.12	35.62	27.82	24.17	22.17	20.98
4,000	96.72	47.49	37.09	32.23	29.56	27.97
5,000	100.19	59.36	46.36	40.28	36.95	34.97
10,000	200.38	118.71	92.71	80.56	73.90	69.93
15,000	300.57	178.06	139.06	120.84	110.85	104.89
20,000	400.76	237.41	185.41	161.12	147.80	139.85
25,000	500.45	296.76	231.76	201.40	184.75	174.81
30,000	601.14	356.11	278.11	241.68	221.70	209.77
35,000	701.33	415.46	324.46	281.96	258.65	244.73
40,000	801.52	476.81	370.81	322.24	295.60	279.69
45,000	901.71	534.16	417.16	362.52	322.55	314.65
50,000	1,001.90	593.51	463.51	402.80	369.50	349.61
55,000	1,102.09	652.86	509.86	443.08	406.45	384.57
60,000	1,202.28	712.22	556.21	483.36	443.40	419.53
65,000	1,302.47	771.57	602.56	523.64	480.35	454.49
70,000	1,402.66	830.92	648.91	563.92	517.30	489.46
75,000	1,502.85	890.27	695.26	604.20	554.25	524.42

Amount borrowed

Monthly payment

half-point increments, you can calculate the approximate payment by averaging monthly payments for two known interest rates.

▶ Example: You know that at 7.5%, the monthly payment for a $10,000 loan over 30 years is $69.93, according to the table. (Earlier in the chapter, the calculated payment was $69.92. The difference comes from the method used in rounding.) The 8.0% table would show that the monthly payment for borrowing $10,000 for 30 years is listed as $73.38. What is the monthly payment for 7.75%? To calculate this payment, add the two known payments and divide by two:

Interest rate: (7.50% + 8.00%) ÷ 2 = 7.75%
Monthly payment: ($69.93 + $73.38) ÷ 2 = $71.66

The 7.75% table would show that the actual payment required is $71.65.

These calculations make the point that payment requirements can be estimated based on variations of the rate, number of years, and amount borrowed. In addition, by changing the variables in the spreadsheet program, you can determine the monthly payment for any interest rate, amount borrowed, or repayment term. This is valuable in analyzing and comparing loans and deciding which arrangement is most suitable.

Comparing Loans

The comparison further helps in determining the true overall interest expense of multiple loans. If you are working with two or more loans and you want to find their average interest rate, you cannot simply add them and divide by the number of loans. The outcome is going to be distorted when the amounts borrowed are different. To determine the average rate, you need to calculate the weighted average; this means that greater weight is given to larger amounts borrowed and less to smaller amounts.

Example: You have two loans outstanding. The first is a $10,000 loan at 7.5%, and the second is an $18,000 loan at 12.0%. What is the weighted average of these loans? To calculate the average, you cannot add together the two rates and then divide by two (producing an average interest rate of 9.75%). Because the amount borrowed at the higher rate is more than the amount borrowed at the lower rate, you know that the weighted average must be greater. To weight the average, add the amounts borrowed and then use the total as the denominator in a fraction for the sum.

BASIC MATH REVIEW

A fraction consists of the top number (numerator) and the bottom number (denominator). To multiply a whole number by a fraction, multiply the number by the numerator and then divide by the denominator. For example, if you want to find 3/8ths of 47:

$(3 \times 47) \div 8 = 17.625$

Proof: To prove this outcome, calculate in the reverse order: Divide 17.625 by 3, then multiply by 8:

$(17.625 \div 3) \times 8 = 47$

Applying the use of the fraction to the calculation for weighted average, first add the two loan amounts:

$10,000 + $18,000 = $28,000

Because fractions are always the same when reduced in size, these expressions can be shown as 10,000/28,000 and 18,000/28,000 or simply as 10/28 and 18/28. They can also be simplified to their lowest form, or 5/14 and 9/14.

BASIC MATH REVIEW

Fractions can be reduced to their lowest common denominator (LCD) to simplify functions using those fractions. The LCD is defined as the smallest equivalent fraction. For example, the fraction 6/10 is equivalent to the LCD of 3/5. To calculate, divide both sides of the fraction by a divisor that goes into both. In the case of 10,000/18,000, start by eliminating the zeros (10/18); next determine what divisor goes into both 10 and 18. These can both be divided by 2, creating the equivalent of 10/18 in the form of 5/9.

The fractions 5/14 and 9/14 are the same as 10,000/28000 and 18,000/28,000. Using the lowest form of the fractions, you can find the weighted average by multiplying the known interest rates by the reduced fractions for the loan amounts. You know that 5/14 of the loan

($10,000) is being paid at 7.5% and that 9/14 is being paid at 12.0%; so the weighted average is:

(7.5% × 5/14) + (12.0% × 9/14) = (2.679) + (7.714) = 10.393%

The weighted average of these two loans is 10.393%. The formula for weighted average is:

Weighted Average

$$[I_1 \times (L_1 \div L_t)] + [I_2 \times (L_2 \div L_t)] = W$$

where: I_1 = interest rate, loan 1
$\quad\quad L_1$ = borrowed amount, loan 1
$\quad\quad L_t$ = total of amounts borrowed
$\quad\quad I_2$ = interest rate, loan 2
$\quad\quad L_2$ = borrowed amount, loan 2
$\quad\quad W$ = weighted average

On a spreadsheet program, enter the following values:

A1	LOAN AMOUNT 1	L_1
B1	LOAN AMOUNT 2	L_2
C1		= SUM(A1 + B1)
A2	INTEREST RATE, LOAN 1	I_1
B2	INTEREST RATE, LOAN 2	I_2
A3		= SUM(A2*(A1/C1))
B3		= SUM(B2*(B1/C1))
C3	WEIGHTED AVERAGE	= SUM(A3 + B3)

▶ Example: We will use the data from the previous example: a $10,000 loan at 7.5% and an $18,000 loan at 12.0%:

	A	B	C
1	10,000	18,000	28,000
2	7.50	12.00	
3	2.679	7.714	10.39

Calculating weighted average is not a complicated process, as long as the relative role of each loan is expressed in fractional form. The total amount borrowed is always the denominator, and each loan represents the numerator.

ANNUAL PERCENTAGE RATE

The term *nominal rate* refers to the stated interest rate. However, the nominal rate is not the same as the annual percentage rate, or APR, which is the actual interest rate you pay with periodic compounding.

▶ Example: You might be offered a working capital loan for one year at 7.5%. A 7.5% nominal rate, compounded quarterly, produces an APR of 7.71%:

$$[1 + (7.5\% \div 4)]^4 - 1 = 7.71\%$$

In some applications of the term, APR includes not only the compound interest per year, but also any fees added to the cost of borrowing money: loan origination fees, points, and service charges. The accurate computation requires the interest to be computed first, and then applicable fees added, and the total dollar value to be divided by the amount borrowed.

Annual Percentage Rate (APR)

$$[(\{[1 + (i \div p)]^n - 1\}\ L) + F] \div L = A-$$

where: i = interest rate
p = periods per year
n = number of periods
L = loan amount
F = fees
A = APR

On a spreadsheet program, enter the following fields:

```
A1 = SUM(I/P) + 1     = SUM(A1*A1)
B1
```

C2	= SUM(B2-1)*L)
D2	= SUM(D2 + F))
E2	= SUM(D2/L)

▶ Example: You borrow $50,000 at a 7.5% rate compounded quarterly. The basic compound rate is 7.71%, as already demonstrated. However, your lender charges a loan origination fee of $400 on top of interest. The APR is calculated as:

$$[(\{[1 + (0.075 \div 4)]^4 - 1\} \times \$50,000) + \$400] \div \$50,000 = 8.51\%$$

The first-year APR is higher than the compound interest rate due to the addition of up-front fees. Subsequent years revert to the calculation involving interest only, unless additional fees are to be assessed according to the contract.

In calculating the APR on any loan, remember that the inclusion of fees varies by lender and state. Some APR calculations are restricted to interest only, and others include fees charged to originate and process the loan.

LOOKING AHEAD

Calculating the interest cost of money is a well-known version of how interest works. The flip side of the same series of equations is the calculation of *return* in various forms. *Return* (also called *yield*) is the outcome calculated on revenues, cash, or invested capital. The next chapter provides calculations and examples for many versions of return.

C H A P T E R 3

Rates of Return

E very manager faces the need to calculate returns on a variety of activities. The most pressing of these is the financial return, that all-important analysis of profitability. The profit, analyzed in comparison to revenues, is the universal test of how well your company performs.

Besides net return, other tests are equally important as measurements of financial performance: return on cash or capital, dividend yield, and comparisons between equity and debt. The return (or yield) is universally recognized for many financial and cash flow–related tests; the range of applications makes the analysis of "return" complex because it has so many definitions. This chapter analyzes and explains the various forms of return and yield in specific categories: revenue and equity, cash flow, capital, debt, and investment.

RETURN ON REVENUE AND EQUITY

Within the range of return on revenue and equity, an array of financial calculations comes into play. Every manager, even those not involved directly in accounting and financial reporting, will end up being involved in the monitoring of business activity, which is invariably expressed in terms of return. Every manager will be judged on the basis of how consistently a return is generated and by how much growth is generated. This is the primary method for making judgments about a manager's success or failure.

Because there are so many variations on return, making clear distinctions is crucial. The two most important distinctions are return on revenue and return on equity. *Revenue*, also called sales or gross receipts, is simply the percentage of net profit. This is one of the most widely used ratios. In comparison, *return on equity* is the percentage of net profit to net worth. The equity (net worth) is also called shareholders' equity or stockholders' equity in corporations.

Net Return on Revenue

Net return on revenue is easy to calculate; however, the numbers used in the calculation can vary, confusing comparisons between companies. Some "net return" calculations are based on net operating profit (profit before nonoperating income or expenses such as interest, capital gains, foreign exchange profit or loss, and tax liabilities). These nonoperating values can be quite large, affecting the change between operating profit and overall net. Other calculations are based on pretax profit, even though a tax liability can be substantial; the after-tax net profit is the so-called net-net, or the bottom line.

The selection of one number over another should be based on ensuring accurate year-to-year tracking. The nonoperating values can distort the profit in years when they are quite high.

▶ Example: A company's operating profit is $5,000 on total sales of $100,000 (5%). In the same year, a large capital gain of $15,000 was also booked when the company sold equipment at a profit. Total pretax profit was $20,000 (20%). The current year's tax liability was $6,000, bringing after-tax profits down to $14,000 (14%). The selection of one of these forms of profit drastically affects net return calculations:

Net operating profit	5%
Net pretax profit	20%
Net after-tax profit	14%

Because net profit can mean different values based on how it is selected, you need to ensure that any comparisons between two different periods or two different companies are truly comparable. Otherwise, any analysis is going to be inaccurate.

Net Return

$P \div R = N$

where: P = net profit
        R = revenue
        N = net return

On a spreadsheet program, enter the following values:

A1 P
B1 R
C1 = SUM(A1/B1)

▶ Example: If net profit is $427,600 and revenue is $5,342,400, the spreadsheet entries are:

A1   427,600
B1   5,342,400

Applying the formula, cell C1 is 0.0800 (8.0%).

Net return is important because it reveals how successfully the company managed costs and expenses during the year. You want to see profits rise with revenue, but just looking at the numbers can be deceptive, which is why the use of formulas is essential. One negative trend to look out for is a falling net return while revenues are rising.

▶ Example: Look at a record of several years' revenues and net profits:

Year	Net Profit	Revenues
1	$427,600	$ 5,342,400
2	461,000	7,616,300
3	494,500	9,827,900
4	507,800	12,625,000
5	527,200	17,570,400

At first glance this record looks impressive. The dollar value of revenues and net profits has been rising substantially every year.

Year	Net Profit	Revenues	Net Return (%)
1	$427,600	$ 5,342,400	8.0
2	461,000	7,616,300	6.1
3	494,500	9,827,900	5.0
4	507,800	12,625,000	4.0
5	527,200	14,310,400	3.7

Although the dollar value of both revenue and net profits rose over
five years, the net return fell by more than 50%. This could be caused
by a higher cost of doing business at a higher volume, or it could be a
sign that costs and expenses are outpacing the growth in revenue.
The answer is worth investigating. The dollar value analyzed without
the net return does not reveal the trend, and the trend does not
always fully explain the underlying cause for the trend. However,
whatever further analysis reveals, the pursuit is worthwhile.

Net Return on Equity

Return on equity is a similar calculation. Net profit is divided by equity.
In the case of net return, both net profit and revenue cover the same
period (e.g., one year's profits are divided by one year's total revenues).
However, in the case of return on equity, the period's net profits are
divided by the ending balance for the year (or quarter). In the first
instance, both values come from the income statement; in the second,
the income statement value (representing a period's activity) is divided
by a balance sheet value (representing the net worth at the end of the
period).

Return on Equity

$P \div E = N$

where: P = net profit
E = equity (net worth)
N = return on equity

On a spreadsheet program, enter the following values:

A1   P
B1   E
C1   =SUM(A1/B1)

▶ Example: Your company reported net profit this year of $428,000. The equity (net worth) as of the end of the year was $5,226,000. Return on equity is:

$428,000 ÷ $5,226,000 = 8.2%

The spreadsheet entries confirm this:

A1   428,000
B1   5,226,000

Applying the formula, cell C1 is 0.0819 (8.2%).

Return on equity shows how effectively your company has been able to put its resources to work in generating profits. This formula is not entirely accurate if the value of equity has changed during the year. For example, if additional stock has been created and sold, both beginning and ending balances of net equity are not representative of the entire year. The net income is income for the whole year, but if equity changes, then its value has to be based on the average for the full year.

▶ Example: Your company began the year with net worth of $4,000,000. On May 1, additional shares of common stock were sold and valued at $1,000,000. On September 1, an additional offering of $500,000 was made. And on November 1, the company bought $274,000 worth of shares and retired them. The year-end balance of net worth was $5,226,000. The value for each month was:

January	$4,000,000
February	4,000,000
March	4,000,000
April	4,000,000
May	5,000,000

June	5,000,000
July	5,000,000
August	5,000,000
September	5,500,000
October	5,500,000
November	5,226,000
December	5,226,000

To find the average, add up the values and then divide by 12 (months).

Simple Average

$$(V_1 + V_2 + \ldots V_n) \div n = A$$

where: V = value

     1, 2 = field number

     n = last number in the field

     A = average

▶ **Expressing the same formula in a simplified form, add up the values for each month and then divide by 12:**

$57,452,000 \div 12 = $4,787,667$

On a spreadsheet program, enter the following values (based on assumed 12 values):

A1	V_1
A2	V_2
FINAL CELL (A12)	V_N
B12	= SUM(A1:A12)/12

The outcome using the 12 values in the example is shown in Table 3-1.

▶ **In the case of the changed value of equity throughout the year, this formula can be proven by multiplying the balance by a fraction for each portion of the year (e.g., four months is equal to the fraction 4/12):**

TABLE 3-1 SIMPLE AVERAGE

Month	A	B
January	4,000,000	
February	4,000,000	
March	4,000,000	
April	4,000,000	
May	5,000,000	
June	5,000,000	
July	5,000,000	
August	5,000,000	
September	5,500,000	
October	5,500,000	
November	5,226,000	
December	5,226,000	4,787,667

4/12 × 4,000,000	=	1,333,333
4/12 × 5,000,000	=	1,666,667
2/12 × 5,500,000	=	916,667
2/12 × 5,226,000	=	871,000
Total		4,787,667

This average is used in the calculation of return on equity to make it representative of the entire year. The average net worth has to be used because both the beginning and ending balances for the year distort the true picture.

▶ Example: The adjusted return on equity is:

$428,000 ÷ $4,787,667 = 8.9%

The formula is adjusted in one specific circumstance. When a corporation has issued redeemable preferred stock (a special class of equity that acts more like a bond than like equity), the formula should exclude its value. This formula produces the net return on equity.

Net Return on Equity

$P \div (E - S) = N$

where: P = net profit

E = equity (net worth)

      S = redeemable preferred stock
      N = net return on equity

On a spreadsheet program, enter the following values:

▶ **Example: Your company has reported net income of $428,000 and had an average equity value for the year of $4,787,667. Return on equity was calculated at 8.8%. However, equity included $300,000 in redeemable preferred stock. On the spreadsheet, enter the values:**

A1   428,000
B1   4,787,667
C1   300,000
D1   = SUM(A1/(B1-C1))

The return on net equity is:

$428,000 ÷ ($4,787,667 − $300,000) = 9.5%

Although the formulas for return on revenue and return on equity are simple, finding the right values is not always as easy. Ensuring the consistency of the values used is a basic requirement for high-quality analysis of financial results.

CASH RETURN AND CASH FLOW

Cash flow is at least as important as profits. This concept refers to how much cash is available to an organization to (1) pay current bills on time, (2) take advantage of discounts or volume purchases, (3) build adequate inventory levels, (4) carry the value of accounts receivable, and (5) pay for expansion of markets or products.

Payback Ratio

Using cash flow as a measurement of investment success, you can measure how long it should take to break even. The *payback ratio* addresses the question, "How long will it take to get back my investment (based on cash flow)?" This issue comes up whenever a business places cash into a new product, for example, or expands geographically. Management needs to know how much commitment is involved. The commitment for expansion is not limited to the cash, but also includes the time needed to recapture that cash.

The payback ratio compares the initial investment to net cash flow. The term *net cash flow* means the total of revenues less costs, expenses, and taxes, all expressed on a cash basis. (Noncash items such as depreciation or accruals are left out of net cash flow.) The formula:

Payback ratio

$$I \div C = R$$

where: I = initial cash investment
  C = net cash flow per year
  R = payback ratio

On a spreadsheet program, enter the following values:

A1   I
B1   C
C1   = SUM(A1/B1)

▶ Example: Your company has invested $235,000 to expand its geographic market over the next year. The question has been raised, "How long will it take to recapture this investment based on increased profits?" The analysis of this plan originally was prepared in the usual forecasting and budgeting model, and it did not adjust to cash-only. A revised forecast estimated that net cash flow per year will average $41,500. Enter these fields on the spreadsheet:

A1   235,000
B1   41,500
C1   = SUM(A1/B1)

The payback ratio is:

$235,000 ÷ $41,500 = 5.7 years

The forecast indicates that it will take 5.7 years to break even on this expansion, based on the forecast model being used. For management, the ultimate decision to proceed or not should rely on whether the forecast is reliable, as well as on whether an investment of $235,000 for nearly six years is prudent. Even if long-term profits will grow beyond the forecast level, management has to be concerned with the level and time of the commitment. This concern makes the payback ratio a valuable test of long-term return on investment.

Cash-on-Cash Return

A closely related test of return is called *cash-on-cash return* (also called equity dividend yield). This is a test of the actual return based on cash flow per year, and the formula is the opposite expression of the payback ratio:

Cash-on-Cash Return

$C \div I = R$

where: C = net cash flow per year
$\quad\quad I$ = initial cash investment
$\quad\quad R$ = cash-on-cash return

On a spreadsheet program, enter the following values:

A1   C
B1   I
C1   = SUM(A1/B1)

▶ Example: Using the previous example, the cash-on-cash return is expressed as a percentage:

$41,500 \div $235,000 = 17.7\%$

Enter these values:

A1   41,500
B1   235,000
C1   = SUM(A1/B1)

Although this is simply the reverse calculation of the payback ratio, it is also revealing. Management knows it will take 5.7 years to recapture its initial investment based on forecast annual cash flow.

This type of information is instructive when making judgments about the level of cash and the time required to recapture it. Cash-on-cash adds to the information by reducing the question to a cash-based rate of return on the investment. This ratio is especially useful when comparing the planned expansion proposal to current operations. If the current configuration is earning net return of 9.0% per year, the expansion program is going to be more aggressive than current income levels. If the cash-on-cash return comes out lower than current net profits, the question has to be raised: "Is this expansion proposal a good idea?"

With the combination of the payback ratio and cash-on-cash return, management can determine (1) the time required to recapture the cash outlay, (2) the cash-based return based on the forecast, and (3) the profitability of the expansion compared to the current profitability of the organization.

In studying and comparing the cash-on-cash return to current net profits, it is not entirely accurate to use the tax-based profits of the organization. Because this includes noncash expenses, it is not comparable to the cash-on-cash return. To make the two sides of the equation comparable, current income should be adjusted to the cash basis. This does not require completely revamping reporting profits; for the purpose of comparisons between the organization's profits and cash-on-cash return, the only recurring noncash expense, depreciation, should be added back in to the reported profits. (Depreciation calculations are explained in Chapter 7.) Here is the formula for cash income:

Cash Income

$I + D = C$

where: I = net income
D = depreciation expense
C = cash income

On a spreadsheet program, enter the following values:

A1   I
B1   D
C1   = SUM(A1 + B1)

Enter these values:

A1   1,450,000
B1   850,000
C1   = SUM(A1 + B1)

Example: Last year's net income was $1,450,600 against revenues of $16,118,000. Net return was:

$1,450,600 ÷ $16,118,000 = 9.0%

The initial comparison between this net return and a planned expansion generating 17.7% cash-on-cash return seems to point to an obvious conclusion: The expansion makes perfect sense. However, annual depreciation expense is approximately $850,000. Applying the cash income formula:

$1,450,600 + $850,000 = $2,300,600

This changes the picture. Now the net return using cash income is:

$2,300,600 ÷ $16,118,000 = 14.3%

Although this adjusted calculation is still below the forecasted 17.7% cash-on-cash return expected from expansion, the cash income is quite close. It raises a new question: "Is the expansion feasible given its proximity to current cash income?" There is some doubt. First of all, the comparison is being made between known historical income and a forecast outcome. If the forecast is off over the next 5.7 years and less additional cash profit is generated, the company might not recapture its investment for many years beyond.

This does not indicate that the expansion is an ill-conceived idea. It does point to the possibility that the risk of leaving that much cash outstanding for so many years may be too high. The judgment call is not merely a comparison between returns of 9.0% and 17.7%. The estimated outcomes are much closer when analyzed on a cash basis.

Management makes better decisions when its information is reliable. The preceding example demonstrates that when current profitability and forecast expansion profitability are both compared on a net cash basis, the likely outcomes are much closer than the original numbers indicated.

RETURNS ON PURCHASES AND SALES

Every organization invests in money in capital assets or marketable securities. Capital assets—equipment, machinery, vehicles, and real estate—are depreciated over a recovery period, and the depreciation is deductible from revenues as part of the income statement. When expenses are taken into account as part of the return calculation, a few variations of return can result: the return on purchase price, return on cash investment, and return on net investment. When you are dealing with the return on an investment that includes income in the form of either interest or dividends, the so-called total return has to include these as part of the equation.

Return on Purchase Price

The *return on purchase price* is a calculation of the return on the entire price, regardless of whether it was partially financed and without considering depreciation and other costs. This calculation also does not take into account the holding period. To calculate, divide the net difference between sale and purchase by the original purchase price.

Return on Purchase Price

$(S - P) \div P = R$

where: S = sales price
P = purchase price
R = return on purchase price

On a spreadsheet program, enter:

A1   S
B1   P
C1   = SUM(A1-B1)/B1

▶ Example: You purchased a capital asset for $16,500 two years ago. This year you sold it for $19,000. The return on purchase price is:

($19,000 − $16,500) ÷ $16,500 = 15.2%

Return on Cash Invested

When you purchase an asset for $19,000 and finance $17,000 of the price, the return on purchase price does not tell the entire story. Obviously, the outcome is different if you pay all cash versus borrowing most of the price. With this in mind, a more reliable calculation is *return on cash invested* (also called return on invested capital).

Return on Cash Invested

$(S - P) \div I = R$

where: S = sales price
       P = purchase price
       I = cash invested
       R = return on cash invested

▶ Example: You buy an asset for $16,500 but finance $11,000; you invest $5,500.When that asset is sold for $19,000, the return on cash invested is much different from the previously calculated return on purchase price. However, this calculation still does not take into account the cost of borrowed money, depreciation, or holding period. Apply the formula:

($19,000 − $16,500) ÷ $5,500 = 45.5%

This outcome measures only the net profit versus cash invested and, because it does not take the entire cash difference or time into account, is not a reliable measurement of profitability on the transaction. However, it is useful in judging the effectiveness of borrowing money to invest. For example, if the transaction had resulted in a loss, then the formula could be used to calculate the negative effects of borrowing money, which becomes useful when a series of similar transactions are compared.

This formula can also be summarized on a spreadsheet. Enter the following fields:

A1   S
B1   P
C1   I
D1   = SUM(A1-B1)/C1

Applying the example, entries are:

A1   19000
B1   16500
C1   5500

Return on Net Investment

The next formula in the progression requires expressing the outcome on a realistic basis, which requires taking costs into account. The net investment is the actual cash put into an investment, adjusted downward for the costs involved. So if you borrow money to finance the purchase, the return has to be reduced by the interest expense related to the loan. The formula for *return on net investment* does that, making the calculation more valuable in comparing two or more outcomes.

Return on Net Investment

$(S - P - C) \div I = R$

where: S = sales price
P = purchase price
C = costs
I = cash invested
R = return on cash invested

▶ Example: If you buy an asset for $16,500 with a $5,500 investment, the return on cash invested when selling for $19,000 (as previously calculated) provides part of the answer, but it does not consider the cost of borrowing money. If interest came to $1,700 in this case, the calculation would have to reduce net return by that amount:

($19,000 − $16,500 − $1,700) ÷ $5,500 = 14.5%

This is considerably lower than the previously calculated 45.5%, which excluded interest. However, the cost of borrowing money is a substantial factor in the calculation of overall return.

This formula can also be reflected in spreadsheet entries:

A1   S
B1   P
C1   C
D1   I
E1   = SUM(A1-B1-C1)/D1

▶ Example: Applying the example, the entries are:

A1   19000
B1   16500
C1   1700
D1   5500

The inclusion of costs is critical to arriving at an accurate formula for the net cash return on an investment. Costs may also include a variety of items beyond interest needed to arrive at the true net difference. In some kinds of investments, the adjustment needs to include the effects of earnings. For example, if you buy shares of a mutual fund with temporarily excess cash, the net return should be adjusted upward for any interest, dividends, or capital gains received during the holding period. The calculation is the same as that to account for costs; however, the added income would be an addition to the cash-based profit rather than a reduction.

INVESTMENT-BASED RETURNS

In addition to calculating return on revenue or capital, you may also need to calculate return on investments in various forms. These calculations cover a range of topics, including dividend yield, current yield, and earnings expressed on a per-share basis.

Dividend Yield

Dividend yield (also called current yield by stock analysts) is the percentage represented when dividend per share is divided by the current price per share.

Dividend Yield

$$D \div P = Y$$

where: D = dividend
P = price per share
Y = dividend yield

▶ Example: You are considering investing in stock currently selling for $52 per share. The company's announced dividend per share is $1.40. Dividend per share is:

$1.40 ÷ $52 = 2.7%

The formula can be summarized on a spreadsheet program, using the following values:

A1   D
B1   P
C1   = SUM(A1/B1)

In calculating dividend yield, remember that the outcome is going to vary every time the price per share changes. Accordingly, this calculation applies in two circumstances. First, when considering investing in shares, the yield applies to the current price. Second, after purchase, the yield you calculated at the time of purchase is the applicable yield, even if price has changed significantly. The higher the price is, the lower the yield will be for a dividend that has not changed.

▶ Example: In the previous example, stock was selling for $52 per share and the dividend yield was 2.7% based on an annual dividend of $1.40 per share. However, if the stock price rose to $55 per share, the yield would fall to 2.5% ($1.40 ÷ $55). If the price per share fell to $50, yield would rise to 2.8% ($1.40 ÷ $50).

The yield an investor earns is based on the price paid per share, and not on the ever changing price per share.

Current Yield

Another form of current yield applies to bonds. This is a more complex calculation because it is based on the changing current value of the bond. A bond may sell at par (100) or at a discount or premium below or above par. This is caused by the changing market interest rate compared to the fixed rate paid by the bond. When bond interest is higher than market rates, the bond is likely to sell at a premium. To calculate the current yield, the nominal (stated) yield is divided by the current value (premium or discount). This produces the *current yield*. A bond selling at par reflects a current yield equal to its nominal yield. However, whenever the current value is above or below, current yield changes.

Current Yield on a Bond

$N \div V = C$

where: N = nominal yield
V = current value of the bond
C = current yield

▶ Example: The 3% bond you purchased for $1,000 is currently selling at a discount of $980. In bond jargon, the bond in this condition is described as "selling at 98." Current yield is:

$3.00 \div 98 = 3.1\%$

If the bond were later to appreciate to 103 (a premium 3% above par, or $1,030), the formula is:

$3.00 \div 103 = 2.9\%$

The formula can also be summarized on a spreadsheet:

A1   N
B1   V
C1   = SUM(A1/B1)

Earnings per Share

A popular investment calculation is *earnings per share (EPS)*, which is simply the company's earnings expressed on a per-share basis. To calculate the ratio, the latest known earnings per year are divided by the number of shares outstanding.

Earnings per Share (EPS)

$E \div S = EPS$

where: E = earnings
S = number of common shares outstanding
EPS = earnings per share

▶ Example: A corporation currently has 1,400,000 shares outstanding. The recently released annual earnings report showed a total of $982,000.

The EPS is:
$982,000 ÷ 1,400,000 = $0.70

The outcome in this example, or 70 cents per share, is valuable when a long-term EPS trend is studied. Most financial ratios are most revealing when you can see whether earnings are improving or declining over many years.

The spreadsheet cell values for this formula are:

```
A1    E
B1    S
C1    = SUM(A1/B1)
```

The EPS is also used in a related formula that is widely used by investors, the *price/earnings (PE) ratio*. This is the price per share divided by earnings per share.

Price/Earnings Ratio

$P \div E = PE$

where: P = price per share
E = EPS
PE = price/earnings ratio

▶ Example: The price per share of stock in a company you are tracking is $35. The most recent EPS is $1.75 (earnings represented $1.75 per share). The PE is:

$35 ÷ $1.75 = 20

To interpret the meaning of the PE, the result, also called the *multiple*, is the number of years of earnings represented by the current price per share. In this example, the multiple of 20 is equal to 20 years of earnings for the company, or simply stated, the number of years of earnings required to pay back the purchase price.

The higher the PE, the greater the market risk. Though opinions vary, it is generally understood that a PE of 25 or below is considered a relatively safe investment, and PEs over 25 are increasingly inflated in value.

The PE can also be summarized on a spreadsheet:

A1   P
B1   E
C1   = SUM(A1/B1)

The PE is widely used as a means for comparing companies to one another or for tracking a company's market risk over many years. It is an especially valuable ratio because it combines a technical indicator (price) with a fundamental indicator (earnings).

A potential problem, however, is a disparity of timing. If the earnings are based on those available three months ago, comparing the reported outcome to the current price could be unreliable or distorted. For this reason, the *forward PE* is often used in place of the more traditional ratio based on potentially outdated earnings. The forward PE is based on currently estimated or expected earnings per share. The formula is identical to that for PE; however, the expected EPS is used in place of the latest reported earnings.

Annualized Return

All return calculations are based on relationships between profits and some form of basis (such as purchase price, equity, or sales). However, the reported return has to vary based on the time period involved. A 4% return over three months is much higher than a 4% return over 15 months. Whenever return applies for a period other than exactly one full year, the rate earned has to be annualized; that is, it must be expressed as if the period in effect were exactly 12 months. For any comparisons between dissimilar holding periods, annualization is essential to ensure accuracy.

To annualize a return, divide the percentage of the return by the holding period expressed in months, and then multiply the result by 12. The use of the number of months is reliable for most applications; however, you can also annualize using weeks or an exact number of days.

Annualized Return

$(R \div H) \times Y = A$

where: R = return
H = holding period
Y = periods in one year (12)
A = annualized return

▶ Example: You have invested funds in two different stocks as part of your business money management program. The stocks both earn 4%. However, one is held for seven months and the other for 15 months. The annualized rate is not the same in both cases. Assuming that annualized return is going to be based on the months each investment is owned, the valued of Y is 12, representing the number of months in one full year. To annualize each of the returns:

7-month holding period: $(4.0 \div 7) \times 12 = 6.9\%$
15-month holding period: $(4.0 \div 15) \times 12 = 3.2\%$

The shorter the holding period, the higher the annualized return and vice versa. The purpose in annualizing is to ensure that comparisons are valid.

▶ Example: In the preceding example, the two 4% returns are not equal because the holding periods are dissimilar. The 7-month return (annualized at 6.9%) was more than twice as profitable as the 15-month return (annualized at 3.2%).

The formula can also be reduced to a spreadsheet calculation (based on the assumed use of 12 months):

```
A1    R
B1    H
C1    = SUM(A1/B1)*12
```

Looking Ahead

Calculating rates of return is not a difficult or complex process. The complexity comes in defining exactly which values to use in the formulas. Annualizing is also crucial to making valid comparisons between two or more outcomes.

In the next chapter, the same basic assumptions and qualifications are applied to the calculation of a topic every manager eventually has to contend with: cash flow and leverage.

C H A P T E R 4

Calculating Breakeven and After-Tax Profit

How do you know whether you are profiting from the use of money? A manager who does not accurately summarize profit and loss can easily fall into a reporting trap—assuming that profits have been earned when, in fact, a net loss has taken place.

This sort of trap occurs when you overlook the effects of hidden costs, inflation, and taxes, all of which affect your estimate of profits. When taken into account collectively, these factors can be significant. To accurately estimate profits, you need to develop reliable methods for estimating hidden costs, inflation, and tax consequences. These are part of any financial summary or cash flow analysis. The profitability of any activity relies on the accuracy of the estimates.

Hidden Costs

Because hidden costs cannot be precisely known in advance, some methodical estimates have to be used to take them into account. The procedure for many unknown hidden costs is to set up a loss reserve.

This reserve is carried as an expense during each period, offset by a reduction in an asset's book value. For example, a bad debt reserve is established to record bad debts on a regular basis even though these will not occur until sometime in the future. The purpose of the reserve is to record an expense in each reporting period rather than all at once.

The accounting theory behind the reserve method is that expenses occur over time, and matters like writing off bad debts should not be reported only in the year when a company realizes that a debt has become uncollectible. So the reserve is created to recognize a portion of future bad debts each year. The principle of recognition is a reference to the accounting period in which an expense is recorded. A bad debt is recorded by reducing the current asset Accounts Receivable by the reserve amount, offset by a current-year expense.

➤ Example: If a company writes off $1,500 per quarter for bad debts, the quarterly entry is:

	Debit	Credit
Bad debt expense	$1,500	
Reserve for bad debts		$1,500

In the asset section of the balance sheet, the bad debt reserve reduces the value of the Accounts Receivable account. If a company has been putting aside a reserve of $1,500 per quarter for the past five quarters, and current Accounts Receivable are $455,000, the status of these two accounts is:

Accounts receivable	$455,000
Less: Reserve for bad debts	− 7,500
Net accounts receivable	$447,500

The company has recognized $1,500 each quarter rather than having a future bad debts expense hit the books all at once. This makes the reporting more orderly and consistent. For example, if the company writes off a bad debt of $6,200 at this point, the write-off goes against the reserve, not against the expense that has been accumulating during the preceding five quarters. The entry to record a bad debt reduces both sides of the asset account:

	Debit	Credit
Reserve for bad debts	$6,000	
Accounts receivable		$6,000

After this entry has been made, the two balance sheet accounts reflect the change:

Accounts receivable	$449,000
Less: Reserve for bad debts	− 1,500
Net accounts receivable	$447,500

By using this system, the company shows a bad debt expense of $1,500 each quarter, and the reserve accumulates until accounts are written off.

The level of bad debts is determined by historical levels. If a company experiences 1.5% bad debts on average, the reserve should be set at that level to anticipate that the trend will continue. As actual bad debts come in higher or lower than the historical level, the reserve should be adjusted.

This summarized version of how hidden costs are estimated and placed into the books is only one way they can be managed. No one likes surprises and managers are no exception. You would not want to have to explain to your boss why your current quarter's profits were unexpectedly reduced by $6,000 because no bad debt reserve had been established.

A similar approach can be used to set up reserves for any number of expenses. In companies with a lot of high-maintenance machinery, a deferred maintenance reserve can be set up to anticipate expensive periodic repairs or replacements. If machinery typically needs to be overhauled every four years, it makes sense to set up a current reserve to book the known future expense every quarter. Equipment may also become obsolete as new models are developed and placed on the market. However, an obsolescence reserve is not normally required because this is assumed to be a part of the depreciation system, which allows the expense deduction of a specified amount per year, based on the method allowed and used. Depreciation is the spreading of the expense of capital assets over several years, and the resulting tax benefits of writing off the expense is also spread over the same period of writing off the asset. Capital assets are booked onto the balance sheet and then depreciated over what is called the *recovery period*. This is a reference to the write-off of the cost of buying and holding capital assets. Over the recovery period, the value of the asset is gradually set up as an expense, and the purchase basis of the asset is reduced. (See Chapter 7 for more information about depreciation.)

So a depreciation system serves two purposes. (1) It sets up a reserve for obsolescence. (2) It provides the method for converting the asset to expense over several accounting periods. The rationale for this is the same as that for setting up a bad debt reserve. Writing off the entire cost of buying new equipment as an expense would distort this year's operating results. By definition, a capital asset lasts for several years, so it is depreciated over a period of time estimated to represent the so-called *useful life* of the asset.

This is not always realistic. For example, in the case of real estate, a purchase has to be placed on the books at the actual purchase price and then depreciated over many years. Two factors distort this procedure.

- First, land cannot be depreciated; so its value remains unchanged for the entire time your company owns it.
- Second, the book value of real estate declines each year as depreciation is recorded, even when the market value of real estate rises. The accounting convention does not allow a company to adjust the net book value (purchase price minus depreciation) to reflect its current value. So these adjustments have to be reported in footnotes. The net book value does not always reflect the reality. Real estate may be worth much more, and some other assets (notably vehicles) might be worth much less. It all depends on how value actually changes in the market, compared to a preestablished depreciation schedule.

▶ Example: Your company has two assets on the books that are valued improperly. Many years ago, the company purchased its headquarters building for $2.6 million. Today, the book value is approximately $1.9 million, net of depreciation. However, the company recently refinanced its mortgage, and the latest appraisal concluded that the property is now worth $4 million. The second asset is a truck purchased for $28,000. Net book value today is $16,000, but, because the newest models provide greater fuel efficiency and lower-maintenance engines, the true market value of the truck is estimated at only $2,000. The adjustments between net book values and market values are:

	Net Book Value	Market Value	Difference
Real estate	$1,900,000	$4,000,000	($2,100,000)
Vehicle	16,000	2,000	14,000

The vehicle's disparity is quite small compared to the real estate property's change between net book value and market value. This is a common problem, caused by the accounting restriction and the unyielding rule that an asset's acquisition value, minus depreciation, must be the reported book value of that asset.

These kinds of disparities in how assets are valued can lead to problems for companies. In the 1980s when leveraged buyouts were popular, some companies were taken over for a price above book value but below their true market value. If management is not aware of the market value of its capital assets, then the entire financial reporting system can deceive rather than enlighten any analyst.

Hidden costs can involve many other sections of a company's financial report beyond such apparent and visible ones like bad debt reserves or accumulated depreciation. A reserve to cover uninsured losses might be needed in a company vulnerable to litigation but lacking complete insurance coverage. The interest expense of long-term financing without a contractual fixed interest rate poses another form of potential future loss. Inadequate cash flow represents a lost opportunity risk because the company will not be able to act if and when expansion opportunities or mergers and acquisitions become possible. Without cash, many opportunities have to be passed up without taking action. So hidden costs come in many forms, and a realistic approach to long-term planning requires the identification of those costs and, when possible, either setting up reserves or changing the current operating model to reduce or eliminate the problem.

Some small companies, for example, have eliminated the expense of chronic bad debts by simply refusing to extend credit to customers. They require all bills to be paid at the time goods or services are delivered. This move is not always practical and invariably leads to the loss of some business; however, if bad debts have impacted profits to the extent that extending credit is no longer affordable, the loss of business becomes more acceptable than growing losses each year. The combined negative impact on profits and cash flow makes decisions like this unavoidable.

THE INFLATION EFFECT

Hidden costs are likely to destroy even the best thought-out long-term forecast and turn would-be profits into losses. Even if your company sets aside reserves for hidden costs, those costs have an eroding effect. One of the most hidden and most destructive of these is inflation.

Many people misunderstand inflation. Some believe that it is caused by rising prices when, in fact, higher prices are a symptom of inflation, not its cause. The confusion was explained many years ago by Roger Blough, CEO of U.S. Steel, who observed that "[s]teel prices cause inflation like wet sidewalks cause rain."[1]

The real definition of inflation is the gradual erosion of purchasing power. As the dollar's value falls, it takes more to buy the same amount of goods or services. For example, one dollar in 1950 was the equivalent of $7.15 in the year 2000.[2]

> **VALUABLE RESOURCE**
>
> The Bureau of Labor Statistics (BLS) provides a free inflation calculator. You can enter any two years to determine how purchasing power changes over time. Go to www.bls.gov/data/inflation_calculator.htm to use the calculator.

This means that you needed $7.15 in 2000 to buy the $1.00 worth of goods you could have purchased in 1950. The difference, or the loss of purchasing power, comes from inflation over 50 years. The annual or

1. Roger Blough, CEO of U.S. Steel, in *Forbes*, August 1, 1967.
2. Bureau of Labor Statistics (www.bls.gov).

quarterly inflation rate is measured by the consumer price index (CPI), published by the Bureau of Labor Statistics. The rate is based on the cost of a basket of consumer goods, calculated against an index level with a percentage of change each year.

Inflation is caused primarily by changes in the money supply. As more money is printed and distributed, its real value declines. Whenever the money supply grows faster than economic growth (normally measured by gross domestic product, or GDP), inflation rises. Excessive levels of money are printed to fund growing government debt or to improve the credit markets, but over the long term, the effects of inflation create the unavoidable deterioration of purchasing power. For managers, inflation is important not only because it affects purchasing power on both a personal and corporate level, but also because it directly affects all calculations of future cash flow and profits.

By definition, the rate of inflation, which is expressed as a percentage of increase in a specified period (month or year, for example) is based on the use of an index developed by the Bureau of Labor Statistics. To calculate annual inflation, subtract the change in the annual index and divide the difference by the earlier year's index level:

Inflation Rate

$(C - P) \div P = I$

where: C = current CPI index
P = past CPI index
I = rate of inflation, CPI

▶ Example: The Bureau of Labor Statistics reported that its index level at the end of 2008 was 210.2. At the end of 2007 it was 210.0, and at the end of 2001 it was 176.7. These values are based on an index of 100 in 1983. Applying the formula to the seven-year change between the end of 2001 and 2008 (using the CPI for All Urban Consumers, also called *CPI-U*):

$(210.2 - 176.7) \div 176.7 = 19.0\%$

The formula can be summarized on a spreadsheet, using the following field values:

A1   C
B1   P
C1   = SUM(A1-B1)/B1

From a business manager's perspective, the consequences of inflation are likely to be far different from the consequences for an individual consumer. This difference lies in the way that one set of inflated prices affects overall costs to produce, market, and sell goods. For example, the consumer is going to suffer from inflated prices of gasoline and may be less aware that gas prices also affect the cost of food, utilities, and even housing. A business manager is likely to be more aware that the overall inflation rate is not equally distributed. As a result, some costs are not as obvious as others. A lending or savings institution with existing contracts on the books for fixed interest income or expense is going to be very sensitive to changes in interest rates. An organization providing nonessential products or services (such as a recreational company, travel or tourism outlet, or hotel chain) will be far more sensitive to the immediate effect of inflation than a company selling necessities. This problem is especially aggravated in times of hyperinflation, when the rate is either out of control or rising rapidly.

In calculating a true breakeven point, inflation has to be brought into the equation. For managers, the concept of breakeven is the identification of the minimum volume of revenues produced to justify an activity. If this forecasting device does not include a factor for inflation, it will be unrealistic, especially for long-term projections.

▶ Example: Your company is evaluating a multimillion-dollar investment in a new product line, and the initial estimates indicate that, if the project is successful, breakeven will occur within five years. The forecasts include a fixed price and fixed-cost assumption and are based on current expense levels. The breakeven sales level on an annual basis is:

Revenues	$14,400,300
Less: Direct costs, 58%	− 8,352,174
Gross profit	$ 6,048,126
Expenses (fixed assumption)	− 6,000,000
Net pretax profit	$ 48,126 (0.3%)

This set of assumptions includes a belief that the expense level and the percentage of gross profit will remain unchanged. The product becomes profitable if and when revenue levels rise above this breakeven.

▶ Example: If revenues were to rise to $30 million per year:

Revenues	$30,000,000
Less: Direct costs, 58%	− 17,400,000
Gross profit	$12,600,000
Expenses (fixed assumption)	− 6,000,000
Net pretax profit	$ 6,600,000 (22.0%)

These assumptions could be accurate assuming that no inflation occurs. However, what if the cost of goods sold were to rise? What if expense levels increase substantially? One of the assumptions used is that the product's price would be fixed to remain competitive with better established brands.

▶ Example: The estimated 22% return is not going to be accurate if the revenues remain unchanged, but, if direct costs were to rise by 8% over 10 years and expenses were to rise by 15%:

Revenues	$30,000,000
Less: Direct costs, 68%	− 20,400,000
Gross profit	$ 9,600,000
Expenses (fixed assumption)	− 6,900,000
Net pretax profit	$ 2,700,000 (9.0%)

This forecast is less satisfying than the previous assumption of 22%, but it might also be more realistic. Given the altered numbers, with inflation assumptions included, this type of exercise should be built into any long-term revenue and profit forecast.

TAXES IN THE PROFITABILITY EQUATION

Besides inflation, the tax reality should be included in forecasts as well—not only in long-range ones but even in those looking out only one year. Remember:

- Taxes apply to all net income from operations.
- In addition to federal income taxes, state tax rates have to be included.
- A forecast is incomplete if it excludes the tax factor in the outcome.

Corporate tax rates apply both federally and in most states. (Four states—Nevada, South Dakota, Texas, and Washington—assess no income tax). As of 2009, the federal rates are:

Taxable Income over	Not over	Tax Rate (%)
$ 0	$ 50,000	15
50,000	75,000	25
75,000	100,000	34
100,000	335,000	39
335,000	10,000,000	34
10,000,000	15,000,000	35
15,000,000	18,333,333	38
18,333,333	—	35

Rates vary by state. Here are some examples:

California	8.84%
Illinois	7.3
Massachusetts	9.5
New Jersey	7.5–9.0
New York	7.1
Virginia	6.0

VALUABLE RESOURCE

To review the state tax rules and conditions in your state, go to the website www.taxfoundation.org.

▶ Example: If your company is based in California and your taxable income is $12 million, your combined taxes will be:

Federal (35%)	$4,200,000
State (8.84%)	1,060,800
Total tax (43.84%)	$5,260,800

The high combined federal and state corporate tax rates create a very different picture than you get from the pretax profit. The after-tax return is the pretax return minus the effective combined tax rate, and this is the number you must use to estimate a realistic income level:

After-Tax Return

$O \times (1 - T) = A$

where: O = operating (pretax) profit
      T = combined federal and state tax rate
        (in decimal form)
      A = after-tax profit

▶ Example: Your company's pretax profit is $12 million. Your federal rate is 35% and your state tax rate is 8.84%. The formula to determine after-tax profit is:

$\$12,000,000 \times (1 - 0.4384) = \$6,739,200$

If this income represented the operating profit on $150 million, the pretax level would be 8% ($12,000,000 ÷ $150,000,000). However, the after-tax return represents only 4.5% ($6,739,200 ÷ $150,000,000).

In evaluating and comparing net return, the use of the after-tax formula makes more sense, especially in states with high tax rates.

The after-tax return can be calculated on a spreadsheet as well:

A1   O
B1   T (IN DECIMAL FORM)
C1   = SUM(1-B1)*A1

▶ Based on our example, this produces the values:

A1   12,000,000
B1   .4384
C1 $6,739.200

The importance of calculating federal and state taxes as part of the analysis and forecasting of revenues and profits cannot be emphasized too much. Taxes are a key factor and play as important a role as that of inflation. However, when you consider the effect of inflation and taxes together in any estimate of profitability, the entire picture is likely to change even more drastically than when one of these is considered alone.

BREAKEVEN CALCULATIONS: INFLATION AND TAXES

As serious as the impact is of inflation and taxes on true profitability, when the two are combined, their effect is substantial. The impact of inflation and taxes on profitability is unavoidable, even though it is not always taken into consideration. Yet this reality is overlooked in a majority of studies, whether they are aimed at long-term financial results or the shorter-term investment returns and cash flow within a single business cycle. As a result, projections lacking consideration of the tax and inflation impact are unrealistic.

Why do taxes and inflation have to be considered together? The argument could be made that, as long as comparisons are made on a like-kind basis, the interaction of taxes and inflation does not matter. In other words, if the inflation and tax factors are excluded in each case, the comparison is still valid. This is not always so, however, for several reasons:

1. *Taxes vary by the state in which the majority of business activity takes place.* So if two companies under review are active in different jurisdictions, the tax impacts will be quite different.
2. *Federal taxes change based on the dollar levels of taxable profits.* As a result, comparisons between companies with dissimilar net profits are invalidated if the tax impact is excluded. Taxes become very important when projecting future growth in profitability. Under a current level of profits, taxes might be insignificant. However, if the assumptions about future growth are correct, then the resulting changes in effective tax rates could make optimistic forecasts of revenues and profits increasingly unrealistic.
3. *Inflation does not impact every organization in the same way.* A study of the elements making up the CPI show that the collective number is the weighted average of many different products in many different areas. Different companies are going to be subject to varying net inflation rates. For example, a company that relies on the

transportation of goods will be more impacted by higher oil and gas inflation than one providing a service sold over the Internet.
4. *Although general assumptions and estimates of inflation can be applied universally, the specific sector has to be considered to determine how much weight to give to inflation.* Assuming that two or more organizations are going to suffer identical inflation is valid only if they are active in the same primary sector.

When you calculate net return based on adjustments for inflation and taxes, the result makes more sense. A detailed analysis has to be made to adjust for varying tax rates by location and income levels, and the assumptions about inflation have to take specific factors into account. Thus, a published annual CPI may be weighted higher or lower based on how the elements of CPI are calculated. (Check the Bureau of Labor Statistics website for a detailed explanation of the components of CPI: www.bls.gov.)

You need to know your net breakeven return to determine whether profits are really profitable. If in fact you are losing net purchasing power after inflation and taxes, then you face a problem. The calculation of breakeven return is based on the combined effects of inflation and taxes:

Breakeven Return

$$I \div (1 - T) = B$$

where: I = inflation rate
T = effective tax rate, including both federal
 and state (in decimal form)
B = breakeven return

▶ Example: Your company invests temporarily available cash in a carefully selected portfolio of money market funds and high-dividend stocks. The portfolio return has averaged 4.5% over the past year, a return that management considers positive. But is it above breakeven? Based on an assumed 3% annual inflation and combined federal and state taxes at 43.84%, breakeven return in this example is:

$$3.0 \div (1 - 0.4384) = 5.3\%$$

Given these assumptions, your company needs to earn 5.3% on the portfolio just to break even. If you earn anything less than this rate, you are losing money on a net-of-inflation and net-of-tax basis. If you duplicate the 5.3% rate, you are simply holding purchasing power at current levels. So reacting to the 4.5% average return as if it were a profit is not realistic.

The formula can be expressed on a spreadsheet, using the following values:

```
A1    I
B1    T
C1    = SUM(A1/(1-B1))
```

The formula is also summarized by various rates of inflation and tax levels in Table 4-1.

The true effects of inflation and taxes make the point that a simple statement of return without these negative impacts does not tell the story. The higher the combined federal and state tax rate is, and the higher the rate of inflation is, the more you need to earn (whether from investments or business activity) to maintain asset value and purchasing power. This raises another important and troubling issue: Does the inflation/tax risk mean you have to take greater risks to avoid losing purchasing power? Whenever your net return falls below the breakeven rate, you need to make some difficult decisions:

1. *Are the assumptions about inflation realistic?* If you are applying an average CPI, does that include elements that do not directly impact your operation? If so, a more detailed study may reveal that a lower rate applies.
2. *Does it make sense to pursue higher profits?* If your current effective tax rate is minimally above the breakeven rate, what happens if higher profits translate to a higher rate? If the improvement in net profits results in a lower net return that is under the breakeven rate, does it even make sense to pursue those higher profits? Avoiding greater profits due to taxes is counter to the basic capitalistic model of commerce, but you cannot ignore facts.

TABLE 4-1 BREAKEVEN RETURN

Effective Tax Rate (%)	Inflation Rate					
	1%	2%	3%	4%	5%	6%
14	1.2	2.3	3.5	4.7	5.8	7.0
16	1.2	2.4	3.6	4.8	6.0	7.1
18	1.2	2.4	3.7	4.9	6.1	7.3
20	1.3	2.5	3.8	5.0	6.3	7.5
22	1.3	2.6	3.8	5.1	6.4	7.7
24	1.3	2.6	3.9	5.3	6.6	7.9
26	1.4	2.7	4.1	5.4	6.8	8.1
28	1.4	2.8	4.2	5.6	6.9	8.3
30	1.4	2.9	4.3	5.7	7.1	8.6
32	1.5	2.9	4.4	5.9	7.4	8.8
34	1.5	3.0	4.5	6.1	7.6	9.1
36	1.6	3.1	4.7	6.3	7.8	9.4
38	1.6	3.2	4.8	6.5	8.1	9.7
40	1.7	3.3	5.0	6.7	8.3	10.0
42	1.7	3.4	5.2	6.9	8.6	10.3
44	1.8	3.6	5.4	7.1	8.9	10.7
46	1.9	3.7	5.6	7.4	9.3	11.1
48	1.9	3.8	5.8	7.7	9.6	11.5
50	2.0	4.0	6.0	8.0	10.0	12.0
52	2.1	4.2	6.3	8.3	10.4	12.5

3. *Can the situation be improved by shifting domicile and markets?* For example, if your company pays taxes in New York, New Jersey, or California, can you take steps to reduce the state tax burden? Can you relocate to Texas, Washington, South Dakota, or Nevada? The question is more complex than simply changing headquarters; the state where revenues are generated is normally where you pay taxes. Consequently, simply moving your offices to a no-corporate-tax state does not necessarily solve the problem. The issue of pursuing a different geographic customer is more complex and difficult, but it should be considered in the mix of possible solutions.

4. *Is it possible to increase your rate of return, whether on short-term investments or on long-term business activity?* In the weak economy of 2008 and 2009, many publicly listed companies were able to improve net profits even when revenues were lower than those of the

previous year. They did so by cutting expenses, which, in most situations, meant cutting jobs. This is not a good idea if you also want to grow; however, applying austerity to the income statement may be aimed at achieving a higher net profit (net of taxes and inflation) without cutting off expansion. Invariably, methods are available to reduce expenses, but only to a degree. The issue always comes down eventually to a decision about appropriate risk levels and margins of profit.

5. *Can the margin of profit be improved?* This is a difficult task and requires taking more risks in the marketplace. How can your competitive stance be improved without exposing your employees, stockholders, and vendors to heightened market risk? The margin of profit can be improved through greater efficiencies in your supply chain, mergers with competitors, or taking greater market risks. Your company has to confront these issues when it finds the current level of net return to be lower than the breakeven return rate.

CALCULATING CASH FLOW

Managers are preoccupied with cash flow, to an even greater extent than with net profits. There are good reasons for this. If your working capital is not strong enough to pay current bills on time or to finance expansion when opportunities arise, then profits showing up on paper are useless. Cash is much more important than profits.

▶ Example: A company reports annual profits of $1.6 million on sales of $20 million in revenues, or 8%. However, current bills are chronically past due for several reasons: Inventory levels are too high, accounts receivable are being collected slowly, and the company has several loans outstanding.

When a combination of mitigating factors erodes working capital, the consequences are negative. Slow payment of current bills leads vendors to place companies on COD status or even to pursue collection, further eroding a company's credit. The company then finds it impossible to get financing. Meanwhile, current obligations for the repayment of principal and interest are absorbing a growing percentage of profits each month. The tendency is that, once cash flow begins to deteriorate, it only gets worse.

To calculate the dollar amount of cash flow each month:

- Begin with the reported net profit.
- Add in noncash expenses and other sources of funds.
- Deduct all payments not reflected in the income statement. Noncash expenses include depreciation as the most important adjustment. If prepaid accounts and reserves have been set up, the current year's expense entries to those accounts should be added back in as well.

Other sources of funds can include proceeds from:

- New loans approved and granted
- Sales of capital assets
- Legal settlements received

Nonincome declines in cash flow include payments made for:

- Purchase of capital assets
- Repayment of loan principal
- Dividends declared and paid
- Legal settlements paid
- Payments to reduce current liabilities

Cash Flow

$$I + (N + L + A + S + O) - (L + A + S + D + O) = C$$

where: I = net income
N = noncash expenses
L = loan transactions
A = capital asset transactions
S = legal settlements and judgments
O = other adjustments
D = dividends paid
C = cash flow

▶ Example: You company has reported current year net profits of $846,500. This includes:

Depreciation	$42,000
Loan proceeds	$10,000
Sale of capital assets	$16,000
Receipt as a legal settlement	$5,000
Other adjustments increasing cash	$2,000
Loan principal repayments	$114,000
Purchase of capital assets	$307,000
Payment of legal judgments	$265,000
Dividends paid	$110,000
Other adjustments	$15,000

Cash flow is calculated as:

$846,500 + ($42,000 + $10,000 + $16,000 + $5,000
+ $2,000) − ($114,000 + $307,000 + $265,000
+ $110,000 + $15,000) = $110,500

Even though the year's profits were $846,500, the net cash flow picture grew by only $110,500. The adjustments are significant because in this situation, management might be considering an expansion plan. The argument might be put forth that, because profits were $846,500, the estimated cost of expansion of $600,000 is easily afforded. When cash flow is reviewed with the adjustments, however, the flaw in this conclusion is apparent. Because so many negatives were involved, the company's cash flow is not adequate to fund the expansion plan.

The calculation of cash flow can be summarized on a spreadsheet. Use the following field values:

A1	I
B1	N
B2	L
B3	A
B4	S
B5	O
B6	= SUM(B1:B5)
C1	L
C2	A
C3	S

```
C4    D
C5    O
C6    = SUM(C1:C5)
D6    = SUM(A1 + B6-C6)
```

▶ These field values, when entered based on the preceding example, produce the following results:

A	B	C	D
846,500	42,000	114,000	
	10,000	307,000	
	16,000	265,000	
	5,000	110,000	
	2,000	15,000	
	75,000	811,000	110,500

Cash flow calculations certainly affect your ability to expand operations or to reduce debt levels, not to mention keeping current obligations current. These calculations should be included in the budgeting process, with expenses expressed in the form of the coming year's budget, revenues in the forecast, and cash flow in the projection. These variations in terminology help to clarify the distinctions between the groups of activity being estimated within the overall budgeting process.

The analysis of return and profit on a realistic basis—the consideration of both inflation and taxes as part of the study—is not just an exercise. In preparation of revenue forecasts, expense budgets, and cash flow projections, making adjustments for inflation and tax assumptions aids in the development of fact-based reports. It also helps to better understand current returns from operations or investments. As long as the operating profit or investment return is not understood in terms of how purchasing power of money is impacted, any analysis (even a comparative analysis) is lacking.

LOOKING AHEAD

The next chapter expands on the concept of using ratios to study the balance sheet, to evaluate working capital, and to compare financial and capital strength. The analysis of the balance sheet as a test of your company's basic financial condition is a sensible way to monitor and score overall performance and the potential for expansion.

C H A P T E R 5

Financial Reporting Formulas: The Balance Sheet

The two primary financial statements used in business are the balance sheet and the income statement. This chapter explains how the balance sheet is put together and provides formulas for the most useful balance sheet ratios.

Even managers who have not had accounting education can master the short list of calculations that reveal the status and financial condition of a business. You do not need to get involved with a highly technical level of analysis; however, you do need to know how to apply about a dozen formulas to compare companies or to evaluate a company's performance over time.

BALANCE SHEET BASICS

The balance sheet gets its name from two of its most important features. First, this report contains the balances of all asset, liability, and net worth accounts as of a specific date, which is the end of a fiscal quarter or year. The date also corresponds to the end date of the same period for which the income statement reports.

► Example: The income statement reports revenues, costs, expenses, and profits for 12 months from January through December 31. The balance sheet released for the same period reflects balances on December 31.

The second source for the name is that the report summarizes a balance between the accounts, based on a formula:

Balance Sheet

$A = L + N$

where: A = assets
      L = liabilities
      N = net worth

► Example: Your company's year-end report includes $14,607,500 in assets. The balance sheet also reports $11,477,250 in liabilities and $3,130,250 in net worth. The formula, applied to these values, is:

$14,607,500 = $11,477,250 + $3,130,250

The formula can also be summarized on a spreadsheet program using the following values:

```
A1    A
B1    L
C1    N
D1    = SUM(B1 + C1) [SHOULD MATCH CELL A1]
```

By definition:

• *Assets* include all properties owned by the company, such as cash, accounts receivable, and capital assets.
• *Liabilities* are the debts held by the company.
• *Net worth* consists of capital stock in corporations (or owners' equity in partnerships and sole proprietorships), as well as any accumulated earnings from past years (called *retained earnings*). Corporations reduce net worth when they pay dividends, and any repurchase of

outstanding shares is also booked into the net worth account as treasury stock.

How the balance sheet balances itself is a mystery to most people who have not been trained in double-entry bookkeeping. The reason the report comes out exactly balanced is not at all mysterious, however. Every entry consists of two equal sides: a debit (left side) and a credit (right side). As long as these entries are made accurately, the sum total of all accounts always comes out to zero. Debits are added and credits are subtracted. Here are some typical entries employing this system:

Description	Debit	Credit
Sales on account	Accounts receivable	Sales
Payment on account	Cash	Accounts receivable
Current debt obligation	Expense	Accounts payable
Payment of the debt	Accounts payable	Cash

This procedure applies to every transaction made in the company books. At the end of the period, the total of all debits is equal to the total of all credits. When the net total of all balance sheet accounts (assets, liabilities, and net worth) is added up, the balance should be equal to the net total of all income statement accounts (revenue, costs, expenses). The balance on each side is the net profit. The income account balances are zeroed out when the books are closed, and the profit is credited (or the loss debited) into the net worth section of the balance sheet. This creates the perfect balance of the balance sheet.

VALUABLE RESOURCE

For a detailed explanation of the double entry system, check http://simplestudies.com/accounting/lessons/p0401.htm.

The components of the balance sheet are broken down into several subcategories, which become very important when balance sheet ratios are developed. These sections are:

• *Current assets,* which are assets that are in the form of cash or that are convertible to cash within one year. The current assets include cash, accounts receivable (net of a reserve for bad debts), notes receivable, marketable securities (investment accounts), and inventory.

- *Capital assets,* also called long-term or fixed assets, are the buildings, vehicles, equipment, and machinery owned by the company, less accumulated depreciation.
- *Intangible assets* are any assets without physical value, including such things as goodwill and covenants not to compete.
- *Prepaid and deferred assets* are accounts set up to be written off over several years. For example, a three-year insurance premium is set up as a *prepaid asset* and one-third moved to the expense account each year. An expense paid before it is due is set up as a *deferred asset,* to be reversed and moved to the expense account in the relevant accounting period.
- *Current liabilities* are obligations that are payable within 12 months: accounts payable, payroll and other current taxes, and 12 months' of payments on long-term notes.
- *Long-term liabilities* are all debts not payable within the next 12 months, including long-term notes or bonds.
- *Deferred credits* are timing differences like deferred assets. For example, if a company receives revenue that will not be earned until the following year, the payment is properly set up as a deferred credit and later reversed and moved to the revenue account.
- *Capital stock* is the initial value of stock issued and outstanding. This value does not change unless additional shares are issued or until the company buys its stock and retires it permanently as treasury stock.
- *Retained earnings* is an account that accumulates each year's profits (as an addition) or losses (as a subtraction) in the net worth section.
- *Other net worth accounts* include nondeductible expenses and dividends.

The purpose of deferred and prepaid accounts is to ensure that all transactions are booked into the right earnings period. One purpose to the accrual system of accounting is to manage transactions to achieve this goal. For example, sales on account (which for many companies are the majority of sales) should be booked into the month when the sale is actually made, even if payment is not received for several months. A liability is booked as an accrual in the period when the goods are received, even if the company does not pay for them for 30 days.

The process of accruals and reversals is the most complex aspect of bookkeeping, even though it is a necessity. Today, with mostly automated entry systems in use, most managers do not need to be concerned with these complexities, except in one respect: The accrual process is not only the most complex area, but also the process where manipulation most often occurs. If a company wants to "cook the books" by over-reporting revenue or deferring expenses, the accrual system can be used to distort the truth. One important service of ratio analysis is in uncovering suspicious or questionable trends. The trend reveals everything, including the distortion of what is taking place. For this reason alone, every manager can vastly improve the ability to study financial reports by applying a few ratios and tracking the trends they represent.

WORKING CAPITAL RATIOS

Balance sheet account balances are used to track some important ratios concerned with working capital (the availability of funds) and capitalization trends (the balance between equity and debt as capital sources for the organization). The first of these two major areas, working capital, involves a few important ratio tests.

First and best-known is the *current ratio*, which is a comparison between total current assets and total current liabilities. Both of these groupings of accounts relate to the availability and use of cash and cash equivalents within the next 12 months. The current ratio is a test of how well a company is able to pay its debts over the next 12 months. The current ratio is calculated by dividing current assets by current liabilities:

Current Ratio

$A \div L = R$

where: A = current assets
L = current liabilities
R = current ratio

▶ **Example: A company reports that its current assets at the end of the year are $415,300 and that its liabilities are $207,900. The current ratio is**

$415,300 \div $207,900 = 2.0$

The formula can also be reduced to a basic spreadsheet program, with the values entered as follows:

```
A1    A
B1    L
C1    = SUM(A1/B1)
```

As a general observation, a current ratio of 2.0 or higher is a good sign, indicating that liquidity is in good shape and that the company is able to fund its debts. A ratio below 1.0 (meaning current assets are lower than current liabilities) is a warning sign, an indication that the level of working capital is a problem and that the company might have problems meeting its obligations in a timely manner. As with all ratios, the current ratio needs to be tracked over a period of quarters or years to see where the trend is headed.

However, trying to accurately interpret the current ratio without analyzing its components can lead to problems. For example, if the company is carrying too much inventory or if it is accumulating accounts receivable without timely collections, the current ratio can appear healthy when, in fact, problems are emerging in managing working capital. So while the current ratio is a worthwhile test to perform, it does not tell the entire story.

The current ratio can also be manipulated to achieve a desired level, making it more questionable as an entirely reliable indicator.

▶ Example: A company has the following values just before closing its books:

Current assets	$702,300
Current liabilities	$412,300

Given these levels, the current ratio is 1.7 ($702,300 ÷ $412,300). However, if the company pays off $75,000 in current liabilities just before closing the books, the current asset and liability levels are changed to:

Current assets	$702,300 − $75,000 = $627,300
Current liabilities	$412,300 − $75,000 = $337,300

Now the current ratio is 1.9, close to the desired 2.0 you look for in the current ratio. Once the current balance sheet has been released, the company can simply allow current debts to rise once again to replace the $75,000 spent. In this situation, the true picture was distorted by timing payments for some obligations, also hiding the real cash flow picture from the analyst.

Because the current ratio is useful, even with its shortcomings, especially as a long-term tracking device for working capital, keep it in your analytical arsenal. However, to best deal with the possible problems not revealed by the current ratio, you may also want to track the *quick assets ratio*, also called the *acid test*.

Quick Assets Ratio

$$(A - I) \div L = R$$

where: A = current assets
I = inventory
L = current liabilities
R = current ratio

▶ Example: The company you are studying reported $415,300 in total current assets, including $206,600 in inventory and $207,900 in liabilities. The quick assets ratio is:

($415,300 − $206,600) ÷ $207,900 = 1.0

The formula can be summarized on a spreadsheet with the following cell values entered:

A1   A
B1   I
C1   L
C1   = SUM(A1-B1)/C1

With the exclusion of inventory, the quick assets ratio is expected (as a general standard) to reside at or above the level of 1.0. This adjustment is valuable in situations where the inventory level is going to vary greatly from one season to another. A retail operation, for example, is expected to have a very high inventory level at the end of the third quarter in anticipation of the holiday season and then a very low inventory level at the end of the first quarter. Because these variations are caused by cyclical factors, not by changes in the business climate, the quick assets ratio can serve as a more reliable quarter-to-quarter predictor than the better-known current ratio.

This ratio is also more reliable because inventory is not as easily converted to cash as other forms of current assets. Even when inventory is depleted through sales activity, it may be first converted to accounts receivable before cash is finally generated. These realities make the quick assets ratio a worthy accompaniment to the current ratio.

RATIOS SHOWING MANAGEMENT OF WORKING CAPITAL

The current ratio and quick assets ratio are general indicators of how well working capital is generated. Such ratios should be tracked over many quarters to see how a trend is developing. Going beyond these initial tests, you need to also determine how effectively management is using its cash, with two specific ratio tests. As explained in the previous section, testing overall current assets may not reveal all you need to know because inventory or accounts receivable levels can be allowed to climb too high. Testing these is an important attribute of working capital analysis. This section presents an explanation of how to test accounts receivable, and a useful inventory ratio test appears later in this chapter.

Testing Accounts Receivable

To test accounts receivable as one component of working capital, you need to decide how effectively the company is collecting its outstanding balances. If the balances are being allowed to remain outstanding for too long, then the trend is negative. A basic way to track this is to *age* the current accounts receivable balances. To age the account, each company owing money is listed on a worksheet and then shown based on how many days the balance has been outstanding. Those between 0 and 30 days are current; those between 31 and 60 days are later but not yet past due. Any accounts over 61 days are past due, and those over 91 days are seriously past due.

Account managers know that the longer accounts remain unpaid, the less likely it becomes that they will ever receive payment. Even accounts that are eventually collected adversely affect cash flow because of the length of time required to make collections.

The aging list can be set up as shown in Table 5-1. The aging list helps to define the time required to make collections, especially when the list is divided into percentages. When the time required is growing, a company can take action to curtail the problem by:

1. Immediately cutting off credit to any company more than 60 days past due.
2. Improving the initial screening process for customers requesting credit, including a review of credit reports for new customers.
3. Accelerating contact policies starting with direct telephone calls to ask for payments.
4. Imposing credit limitations for high-volume customers, especially those that are slow to make payments.

These measures will prevent the problem from worsening and may even prevent future bad debts. However, the overall credit and collections situation can be distorted by only a few high-volume customers. In periods when sales volume is rising quickly, the relationship between the granting of credit and collections tends to change as well. One way to maintain control over the problem of working capital during an expanding market period is to track the days' sales outstanding.

The related ratio tracks sales on a full-year moving basis (continually updating the full 12 months' sales total) and then comparing that average to the changing balances of accounts receivable. To calculate, first determine the revenue total for the past full year, restricting this total to sales made on account, excluding cash paid at the time of the sale. Doing this requires maintaining a running tally. Each day's new credit-based sales are calculated by adding the latest day and dropping the oldest day. To make this calculation easier, you can track sales on a 52-week or 12-month basis. In this alternative, add the latest week's (or month's) sales to the running total and subtract the oldest. Either way,

TABLE 5-1 ACCOUNTS RECEIVABLE AGING LIST

Name	Total	31–60	61–90	Over 90
Percentage	100.0%	____ %	____ %	____ %

you continually end up with a full year's updated revenue total. Then apply this information in the formula:

Days' Sales Outstanding

$R \div (S \div 365) = D$

where: R = accounts receivable balance

S = one year's sales on credit

D = days' sales outstanding

▶ Example: Your company's sales on credit for the past full year have been $9,415,800. The current balance of accounts receivable is $1,042,700. To calculate the days' sales outstanding using the formula:

$1,042,700 ÷ ($9,415,800 ÷ 365) = 40

This calculation reveals that the average account remains outstanding for 40 days.

Given that some receivables are paid very fast and some remain outstanding for a long time, this outcome is not surprising. As a yardstick of how effectively outstanding bills are being managed, you would hope to see this number fall as steps are taken to speed up collections. When the number begins to rise, notably during periods of revenue expansion, it is a warning sign that working capital is not being managed well.

The formula can also be reduced to a spreadsheet program using the following values:

A1   R

B1   S

C1   = SUM(A1)/(B1/365)

Testing Interest Coverage

Another valuable test of working capital management is *interest coverage*. The ratio relates the cash available before paying interest and taxes to the interest a company has to pay on its existing debt. Lenders sometimes use the margin of safety in cash levels to determine how well a company is able to repay a loan. The calculation begins with EBITDA, an acronym meaning *earnings before interest, taxes, depreciation, and amortization*. Put another way, EBITDA is the cash-basis operating income. It excludes noncash expenses (depreciation and amortization) and is the value you find before deducting interest expense and taxes. The formula for EBITDA is:

EBITDA

$$N - (I + T + D + A) = E$$

where: N = net income
I = interest expense
T = taxes
D = depreciation
A = amortization
E = EBITDA

➤ Example: A company reports a bottom-line net income of $1,680,000. However, this figure includes interest expense of $115,200, taxes of $712,300, depreciation of $186,000, and amortization of $2,400. EBITDA is:

$1,680,000 − ($115,200 + $712,300 + $186,000 + $2,400) = $664,100

On a spreadsheet, calculate EBITDA by entering:

A1   N
A2   I
A3   T
A4   D
A5   A
A6   = SUM(A2:A5)
B1   = SUM(A1-A6)

The calculated EBITDA is a somewhat problematical value in financial analysis. It is going to vary considerably depending on such factors as the level of depreciation and taxes, making comparisons between different companies very difficult. However, for the purpose of calculating interest coverage as a test of operating cash-based income versus interest expense, it is a useful component in the formula:

Interest Coverage

$$E \div I = C$$

where: E = EBITDA
       I = interest expense
       C = interest coverage

▶ **Example: Using the previously calculated values, interest coverage is:**

$2,695,900 ÷ $115,200 = 23.4%

This can also be summarized on a spreadsheet program:

```
A1    E
B1    I
C1    = SUM(A1/B1)
```

The ratio is expressed as the number of times interest expense represents EBITDA. This is a valuable calculation when a company's ability to repay is compared to a standard level used by a lender, as well as to the changes this ratio produces as the working capital picture changes over time.

CAPITALIZATION RATIOS

One of the most overlooked areas of financial analysis is capitalization—the types of financing a company uses to fund operations and growth. There are two types of capitalization: equity and debt. *Equity capitalization* is the value of issued-and-outstanding stock and retained earnings, and *debt capitalization* consists of long-term loans, notes, and bonds—in other words, borrowed money.

The higher the level of debt capitalization, the higher the level of profits that have to be spent in debt service, that is, the repayment of loans. The higher the interest a company has to pay, the less capital remains for expansion and dividends. So as debt rises, the relative impact of equity declines and stockholders have less of a chance of future growth. From a manager's point of view, increasing debt means more negative impact on cash flow. At some point, the level of debt can take on such a prominent role that it becomes impossible ever to reverse the trend.

Growing levels of debt are a huge problem for any company interested in growth and in maintaining a return on revenues and equity. For this reason, analyzing and tracking the trend in total capitalization is one of the most important and revealing tests of a company's health that you can perform.

For a manager, controlling debt is simply good cash flow control. As an investor or potential investor, observing the long-term trend tells you whether the company is growing in positive directions or allowing itself to be gradually consumed by growing debt.

Debt Ratio

The most effective test of how a company is financing its operations—and of the trend underway—is to monitor the *debt ratio*. This is a test of the level of debt as a percentage of total capitalization. The formula tracks this on a percentage basis:

Debt Ratio

$D \div T = R$

where: D = long-term debt
T = total capitalization
R = debt ratio

▶ Example: A company you are tracking reports total capitalization (in millions of dollars) of $42,950. Long-term debt is $13,030. The debt ratio is:

$42,950 \div $13,030 = 33.0\%$

This ratio can also be tracked on a spreadsheet using the following cell values:

A1   D
B1   T
C1   = SUM(A1/B1)

The example demonstrates that the company is employing one-third long-term debt and two-thirds equity to finance operations. Is 33% too high? That depends on the industry standard and other factors. For example, if the company is in an industry demanding high inventory levels or the purchase of capital assets every year, a relatively high debt ratio has to be expected.

The most important test is the trend, not just one year's debt ratio. Is the company maintaining the same level (or a declining level) of debt as a percentage of total capitalization each year? Is the relationship between debt and equity remaining the same or declining while revenue and profits are growing? One danger sign is a growing debt ratio during periods of expansion. In the worst case, revenues grow every year and the debt ratio also grows, while net profits remain the same or decline. That is a sign of poor cash flow management.

The debt ratio also should be tracked, along with the current ratio, as a comprehensive test of management and its cash flow policies. Knowing that investors and analysts pay a lot of attention to the current ratio while too often overlooking the debt ratio, company management often finds it tempting to use long-term debt to artificially bolster the current ratio. This ploy creates the impression that the company is managing cash flow effectively when it is actually losing control.

Example: A corporation has reported net losses in the past three years, but it has managed to maintain a current ratio of 2. Based on this, some analysts are confident that management is maintaining effective working capital levels. But a more in-depth analysis reveals the opposite. The numbers (in millions of dollars) reveal:

Year	Net Loss	Current Assets	Current Liabilities	Long-Term Debt	Total Capitalization
1	(4,889)	16,500	8,007	33,006	101,550
2	(2,006)	27,455	13,550	44,615	105,153
3	(10,588)	41,060	20,625	56,673	101,623

An initial analysis, limited only to a study of current ratio trends, reveals the following positive outcome:

Year	Current Assets	Current Liabilities	Current Ratio
1	16,500	8,007	2.1
2	27,455	13,550	2.0
3	41,060	20,625	2.0

This outcome meets the criteria for the current ratio, and at this point many analysts would end their analysis of cash flow control. However, when you study the debt ratio for the same period, you find:

Year	Long-Term Debt	Total Capitalization	Debt Ratio
1	33,006	101,550	32.5
2	44,615	105,153	42.4
3	56,673	101,623	44.8

This analysis demonstrates that the debt ratio moved significantly higher even while the current ratio remained steady. During periods of net losses, you would not expect to be able to maintain as healthy an outcome, but it is clear that something else was going on in this example. The level of current assets rose at about the same dollar amount as long-term debt each year. The company was committing itself to long-term loans or bonds and using the funds to increase current assets or decrease current liabilities, maintaining the current ratio level even while long-term debt was growing.

Without a specific example of how long-term debt and current ratio can be controlled, this explanation might not seem relevant. However, examples can be found in the historical financial reports of listed companies.

▶ Example: Looking back to the period between 1999 and 2002, Motorola (listed under the symbol MOT) lost a combined total of nearly $4.3 billion; however, the company was able to hold its current ratio steady between 1.2 and 1.8. A study of the actual reported numbers shows how this was accomplished (all numbers are in the millions of dollars):

Year	Net	Current Assets	Current Liabilities	Current Ratio	Debt Ratio
1999	$ 817	$16,503	$12,416	1.3	15.3
2000	1,318	19,885	16,257	1.2	19.2
2001	(3,937)	17,149	9,698	1.8	39.3
2002	(2,485)	17,134	9,810	1.7	40.6
Total	(4,287)				

During a four-year period, the company reported net losses of $4.3 billion but maintained (and even improved) its current ratio. This was accomplished by increasing the long-term debt level; at the same time, the debt ratio grew from 15.3% to 40.6%. This finding does not necessarily mean that Motorola's management intentionally manipulated the outcome to maintain the ratio, and, under the accounting rules, there is nothing illegal about increasing debt levels. However, the outcome kept the current ratio at an acceptable level, which was artificial when the long-term consequences were considered. Although Motorola reduced its debt ratio to about 30% by the end of 2008, it remains at twice the level it reported in 1999.

The conclusion: Ratios should be studied over a number of years and in some cases (such as in working capital and capitalization analysis) reviewed in conjunction with other financial ratios. The collective value of studying the debt ratio and current ratio together is much greater than tracking either one in isolation.

Debt Coverage Ratio

A related test is intended to track a company's ability to make debt payments from current levels of net income. The *debt coverage ratio* is a test of both cash flow and capitalization. The formula compares the total of debt payments (including principal and interest) to net operating income for the same period:

Debt Coverage Ratio

$I \div D = R$

where: I = net income
D = debt service
R = debt coverage ratio

▶ Example: Net income for a full year was recently reported as $12,415, and over the same period the total of principal and interest on outstanding loans was $9,516. The debt coverage ratio was:

$12,415 \div \$9,516 = 1.31$

Lenders use the debt coverage ratio and its trend over time to judge how well a company is able to afford repayments of loan commitments.

This ratio, like all others, should be tracked over many years to judge whether the situation is getting better or worse. The lower the factor is, the worse the cash flow health is of the company. In other words, if 100% of net profits were used to make loan payments, the debt coverage ratio would be 1.00.

The formula can be tracked using a simple spreadsheet program:

```
A1      I
B1      D
C1      = SUM(A1/B1)
```

Liability-to-Asset Ratio

A final ratio is the *liability-to-asset ratio*, which involves dividing total liabilities by total assets. This provides an interesting variation on both current ratio and debt ratio, but it is not widely used because it involves all assets and liabilities. Any change in an account affects and perhaps distorts the trend. For example, if the company sells a large capital asset for more than book value, the total value of assets is increased (cash is received above the equipment's book value). At the same time, any remaining liability for the equipment is instantly eliminated. As long as the relative levels of assets and liabilities remain the same, the formula can be a useful indicator, but not as valuable as current ratio combined with debt ratio. The outcome of this ratio shows how well the level of assets are funded by liabilities (with the remaining level funded by equity). In this regard, the liability-to-asset calculation is similar to the debt ratio.

Liability-to-Asset Ratio

$L \div A = R$

where: L = total liabilities
       A = total assets
       R = liability-to-asset ratio

▶ Example: A company's total assets are reported as $1,443,016 and its liabilities are $982,663. The liability-to-asset ratio is:

$982,663 \div $1,443,016 = 68.1\%

The percentage of debt-based funding is 68.1%. This is not the same as capitalization, however, which compares only long-term liabilities and equity capital.

The formula can also be summarized on a spreadsheet:

```
A1    L
B1    A
C1    = SUM(A1/B1)
```

COMBINED RATIOS

In addition to ratios using only balance sheet accounts, many financial ratios combine balance sheet accounts in comparison with the results reported on the income statement. Two turnover ratios are noteworthy: inventory turnover and a comparison between sales and capital (fixed) assets.

Inventory Turnover

Inventory turnover compares the average inventory for the year to the cost of goods sold for the entire period. In developing average inventory, the level of change during the year should dictate how it is calculated. For example, if the inventory levels remain fairly consistent throughout the entire year, a beginning and ending balance can be added and divided by two. When levels change significantly depending on the calendar cycle, use either quarterly inventory levels or even monthly levels, depending on the degree of change.

The ratio estimates the level of cash committed to maintaining required inventory levels, with the intention of indicating when levels should be reduced to improve cash flow. If the company is maintaining inventory at a higher level than required, it not only ties up cash; it is also spending too much money on transportation, insurance, property taxes, warehouse labor, recordkeeping, interest, and the danger of deterioration, damage, theft, and obsolescence. Keeping inventory turnover at a minimum required level based on sales volume for the season saves both cash flow and profits.

Inventory Turnover

$$C \div [(B + E) \div p] = T$$

where: C = cost of goods sold
     B = beginning inventory
     E = ending inventory
     p = number of periods in the average
     T = inventory turnover

▶ Example: A company has reported cost of goods sold for the past fiscal year of $4,500,600. The inventory level at the beginning of the year was $702,400 and at the end of the year was $785,700. Determining that the monthly changes in inventory were not seasonally great, the calculation is performed using beginning and ending inventories only:

$4,500,600 \div [($702,400 + $785,700) \div 2] = 6\%$

The average inventory was "turned" (replaced) six times during the year. On average, the company maintains two months' worth of inventory on hand. This calculation is valuable as a means of tracking inventory management. If the number of turns begins to decline, inventory levels are rising relative to the cost of goods sold. If levels of two months' worth of goods are considered reasonable, a turnover rate below 6 would be a negative trend.

The formula can be summarized in a spreadsheet program using the following cell values:

A1   C
B1   B
B2   E
C2   = SUM(A1/((B1 + B2)/P))

▶ Example: In the preceding example, the cell values are:

A1   4,500,600
B1   702,400
B2   785,700
C2   = SUM(A1/((B1 + B2)/2))

If you determine that inventory needed to be averaged in greater detail, the B column would include quarterly inventory levels in cells B1 through B4, and the value of p would be 4. If monthly averages were to be used, the monthly inventory totals would be entered in cells B1 through B12, and p would be 12.

Fixed Asset Turnover

The *fixed asset turnover* ratio analyzes a relationship between capital investment and sales generation. It is applicable only to companies in which a direct relationship exists between capital investment and the generation of income. So an accounting firm would not use this ratio to track its investment in office equipment and furniture. However, a contractor would be likely to use it to track developments in its investment in equipment used on the job. The ratio is applied to judge whether investment over time is profitable. For example, a decline in the turnover of sales to fixed assets indicates a trend toward less efficiency.

Fixed Asset Turnover

$S \div [(B + E) \div p] = T$

where: S = sales
B = beginning fixed asset value
E = ending fixed asset value
p = number of periods in the average
T = fixed asset turnover

▶ Example: Your company reports sales last year of $8,005,400. The account value of fixed assets at the beginning of the year is $1,008,900 and at the end of the year, $1,188,000. Using only two periods per year to find the average value of fixed assets, the formula for fixed asset turnover is:

$8,005,400 \div [($1,008,900 + $1,188,000) \div 2] = 7.3\%$

Fixed assets were turned an average of 7.3 times during the year; in other words, the sales level generated by capital investment was 7.3 times that investment. A decline in the number of turns would indicate reduced efficiency resulting from overinvestment in fixed assets.

However, this conclusion is relevant only if the nature of the company and the type of sales can identify a direct relationship between fixed assets and sales generation.

The formula can be reflected using a spreadsheet program, with cell contents very similar to those for inventory turnover. In the case of fixed asset turnover, cell contents are:

A1   S
B1   B
B2   E
C2 = SUM(A1/((B1 + B2)/P))

▶ Example: In the preceding example, the cell values are:

A1   8,005,400
B1   1,008,900
B2   1,188,000
C2 = SUM(A1/((B1 + B2)/2))

If you prefer using a greater number of asset values for the year, the B columns can be adjusted as well as the value of p. For example, if you purchased or sold substantial portions of overall fixed assets during the year, you would have to create an accurate average by using a greater number of account value entries.

LOOKING AHEAD

The balance sheet ratios collectively summarize working capital status and trends, as well as overall capitalization. These are crucial trends to track. Combined ratios can also provide early warning signals when either inventory or fixed asset investment levels begin moving in a negative direction. Continuing the analysis of ratios, the next chapter focuses on the income statement and explains a range of tests you can apply to evaluate profitability and internal controls.

CHAPTER 6

Financial Reporting Formulas: The Income Statement

Whereas the balance sheet reports balances of asset, liability, and net worth accounts at the end of the period, the income statement summarizes the transaction activities *during* the period: revenue, cost of goods sold, expenses, nonoperating transactions, and net profit. The balance sheet and income statement are always released together, and the period covered by the income statement must end on the same date as the reporting period of the balance sheet. This is the end of a fiscal quarter or fiscal year. For example, when the income statement covers the period of January 1 through December 31, the balance sheet published at the same time has to report balances as of December 31.

The income statement (also called *profit and loss statement*) includes, in most instances, *accrued* revenue, costs, and expenses. Very few companies report on the cash basis because that system does not reflect an accurate picture or status of the business. Accruals are essential to record all transactions in the proper period. Revenue has to be shown during the period it was earned, not in the period received, and costs and expenses have to be shown in the period incurred, not in the period paid.

▶ Example: A company reports major fourth quarter earnings over $16 million, but at the end of the year about $11 million in accounts receivable remain outstanding. Reporting on a cash basis would underreport revenue by $11 million because those sales were earned in the fourth quarter. Payment will not be received until later, but under the accrual system they are properly reported in the fourth quarter.

▶ Example: At the end of the fiscal year, a manager notices that the accounts payable total is quite high: $4,822,000. If the year's income statement were prepared on the cash basis, the expenses for the year would be underreported by that amount. The expenses were incurred in the fourth quarter, even though the bills will not be paid until later. Under the accrual system, the accounts payable are set up to reflect incurred expenses.

The accrual entries in these examples set up an accounts receivable offset by reported revenue, and an accounts payable liability offset by expenses:

Account	Debit	Credit
Accounts receivable revenue	$11,000,000	$11,000,000
Expense accounts payable	$ 4,822,000	$ 4,822,000

These simplified account entries increase both current assets and current liabilities as offsets to the income statement entries for revenue and expenses. By booking (or, in accounting terms, *recognizing*) these transactions with accruals in their proper periods, the income statement is accurate.

The accrual system is essential to the proper presentation of the range of transactions in the period covered by the income statement. However, because results can also be affected by simply making an accrual journal entry, the methods of reporting have to be carefully controlled and audited. Publicly traded companies are required to undergo audits and to certify that the final versions of financial statements are accurate. Without the independent oversight from an auditing firm, it would be possible to modify financial reports to look positive even when the true outcome is bleak. So a premise for all managers in reviewing financial statements is to realize that accurate reporting relies on the integrity and thoroughness of the independent audit. This is not an absolute guarantee, as history has proved (recall the case of Enron as well as dozens of others where audits failed to ensure accurate financial statements). However, even with its flaws the system in place for audit review is the best available method for preparation of financial reports. Even with the flaws in the U.S. system, it is probably the most reliable and accurate accounting process in the world.

INCOME STATEMENT BASICS

An *income statement* is a series of summarized account totals for a specified quarter or year. The report moves from top to bottom, beginning with revenue and subtracting a series of costs and expenses. The sequence of reporting is:

Revenue
Less: Direct costs
Equals: Gross profit
Less: Expenses
Equals: Net operating profit
Plus or Minus: Nonoperating income or expense
Equals: Pretax net profit
Less: Income taxes
Equals: Net after-tax profit

This series of steps is used by virtually all companies.

▶ **Example: The fiscal year 2009 report for Microsoft showed the following income statement results (in millions of dollars):**[1]

Revenue	$58,437
Less: Direct costs	34,044
Equals: Gross profit	$24,393
Less: Expenses	4,030
Equals: Net operating profit	$20,363
Plus or Minus: Nonoperating income or expense	542
Equals: Pretax net profit	$19,821
Less: Income taxes	5,252
Equals: Net after-tax profit	$14,569

1. Source: www.microsoft.com/msft/earnings.

The components of the income statement can be further broken down into a series of formulas:

Gross Profit

$$R - C = G$$

where: R = revenue
C = direct costs
G = gross profit

In this chapter, the spreadsheet entries are provided using a vertical format rather than horizontal. This conforms to the income statement reporting format, from top to bottom. The spreadsheet entries for gross profit are:

A1   R
A2   C
A3   = SUM(A1-A2)

Operating Profit

$$G - E = O$$

where: G = gross profit
E = expenses
O = operating profit

The spreadsheet entries:

A3   G
A4   E
A5   = SUM(A3-A4)

Pretax Net Profit

$$O + (-) N = P$$

where: O = operating profit
N = nonoperating
income or
expense (net

income added,
net expense
deducted)
P = pretax profit

The spreadsheet entries in this situation include *subtracting* the net nonoperating expense. In the case of a net income, it is added:

```
A5    O
A6    N
A7    = SUM(A5-A6)
```

Net After-Tax Profit

$P - T = Z$

where: P = pretax profit
T = income tax liability
Z = net after-tax profit

The spreadsheet components:

```
A7    P
A8    T
A9    = SUM(A7-A8)
```

The formula for the complete income statement can also be summarized.

Income Statement

$R - C = G$
$G - E = O$
$O - N = P$
$P - T = Z$

where: R = revenue
C = direct costs
G = gross profit
E = expenses

O = operating profit
N = nonoperating income or expense
P = pretax profit
T = income tax liability
Z = net after-tax profit

On the spreadsheet:

A1   R
A2   C
A3   = SUM(A1-A2)
A4   E
A5   = SUM(A3-A4)
A6   N
A7   = SUM(A5-A6)
A8   T
A9   = SUM(A7-A8)

▶ **Example: Entries with the Microsoft example are:**

A1   58,437
A2   34,044
A3   = SUM(A1-A2)
A4   4,030
A   5 = SUM(A3-A4)
A6   542
A7   = SUM(A5-A6)
A8   5,252
A9   = SUM(A7-A8)

Revenue	$58,437
Less: Direct costs	34,044
Equals: Gross profit	$24,393
Less: Expenses	4,030
Equals: Net operating profit	$20,363
Plus or Minus: Nonoperating income or expense	542
Equals: Pretax net profit	$19,821
Less: Income taxes	5,252
Equals: Net after-tax profit	$14,569

This format can be shifted over to the second column (B) and the first column used to label entries by name. An example of this is shown in Table 6-1, the result of changing calculation labels to B in place of A. The format can then be expanded to make comparisons between quarter and year or between two fiscal years. It can also be used to calculate dollar and percentage outcomes (as explained in the next section).

DOLLAR AND PERCENTAGE REPORTING

Income statements are summarized in dollar values, and, in the case of large dollar amounts, the dollar values are expressed in millions of dollars. This makes the information more digestible. In the Microsoft example, the revenue of $58,437 (in millions) is easier to comprehend than the full dollar value (rounded) of $58,437,000,000.

Statements are further reduced to a shorthand reporting format using percentages. This enables you to review not only the dollar values but the relationship between the various components of the statement and the top line, revenue. The formula for reducing each component to a percentage form is:

TABLE 6-1 INCOME STATEMENT

Microsoft Corporation
Income Statement
For the fiscal year ended June 30, 2009

	($ millions)
Revenue	58,437
Direct costs	34,044
Gross profit	24,393
Expenses	4,030
Net operating profit	20,363
Other income or expense	542
Net pretax profit	19,821
Income taxes	5,252
Net after-tax profit	14,569

Percentage of Revenue

$C \div R = P$

where: C = income statement component
     R = revenue
     P = percentage

On a spreadsheet (based on assumption that column B contains dollar values):

```
C1    100.0
C2    = SUM(B2/B1)
Cx    = SUM(Bx/B1)
```

Applying this formula to the previous example, the outcome will look like the income statement in Table 6-2.

This combination of dollar values and percentages allows managers to use the two shorthand methods (abbreviated dollar values in millions and percentages compared to revenue) to very quickly make judgments

TABLE 6-2 INCOME STATEMENT

Microsoft Corporation
Income Statement
For the fiscal year ended June 30, 2009

	($ millions)	(%)
Revenue	58,437	100.00
Direct costs	34,044	
Gross profit	24,393	41.74
Expenses	4,030	
Net operating profit	20,363	34.85
Other income or expense	−542	
Net pretax profit	19,821	33.92
Income taxes	5,252	
Net after-tax profit	14,569	24.93

about the company's operating results. These judgments can be applied between:

- Fiscal quarters
- The quarterly and annual results
- Two or more fiscal results
- Two or more companies in the same industry
- Two or more companies in different industries
- Actual results and the forecast of revenue or budget of expenses and net income

This multitiered analysis facilitates and expedites the process. It also provides a way to quickly spot the red flags of an outcome that makes no sense. For example, if revenue has been growing each year by 5% and the current year shows a jump of 35%, what has taken place? This could be caused by the manipulation of the results (such as booking revenue too early). However, the explanation could also be more benign.

- If the company acquired another organization during the year, all results (revenue, costs, expenses, and profits) are going to depart from an established trend.
- There could have been an accounting valuation change during the year or by a one-time accounting adjustment, called an *extraordinary item*.

Whenever you see unusual or unexpected results to any part of the income statement, whether positive or negative, look for an explanation. If the explanation makes no sense or is not offered, that is the worst type of red flag, indicating deception. This is a rare event, but it can occur. You have the right as a shareholder or potential shareholder to get the answer. The object lesson for this was the well-known case of Enron. Management's explanations simply made no sense, and unfortunately many analysts (including professionals) just didn't pursue the issue. The bottom line is an easy one: Explanations for unusual results should be clear and should make sense. If they do not, the lack of clarity could be a sign that management is not coming clean.

An examination of trends is a valuable management tool, and it requires review of several years' worth of results. You need to look at three years at least, although the longer the period you review, the better.

Ten years of income statements, if available, give you a healthy time period to study the trends in revenue, costs and expenses, and profits. Here are some cautionary points about trends:

1. *Trends are invalidated by mergers or sales.* Any trend involving revenue and profits remains valid only as long as the company's status remains unchanged. In other words, the same subsidiaries are owned throughout the period, and there are no mergers or sales. As soon as an operating segment is sold, all existing trends have to be recalculated, excluding that segment. Any mergers or acquisitions also require the recalculation of trends to ensure that the outcome is valid.

2. *Trends tend to level off over time, so maintaining the same level of growth is not likely.* Statistically, no trend is going to continue in a straight line indefinitely. A year-to-year increase in the dollar amounts of revenue or net profits might continue, but over time that will represent a diminishing percentage increase over the previous year. This occurs because the base changes each time the beginning value (revenue or profits, for example) grows.

▶ Example: A 10 percent growth in a $1,000 starting point equals $100, and the new base becomes $1,100. If the following year's growth remains at $100, it represents only 9.1% ($100 ÷ $1,100).

3. *The trend is only as reliable as the numbers.* If the numbers used as the base for trends are correct, then the trend is a reliable summary of what is taking place. However, if the numbers are wrong, so is the trend. This is one reason that manipulation of the financial results is so destructive. If revenue is booked a year early or if expenses are deferred a year, the trend is not at all accurate.

4. *Trends can be expressed in many ways, including as an annual percentage of change or as a moving average.* The right way to express a trend depends on what is being reported. Charts showing annual *changes* in dollar values are reliable because they are not distorted by the statistical oddity of consistent dollar values and declining percentage growth. The formula for percentage change from year to year is commonly used:

Percentage Change

$(N - O) \div O = P$

where: N = new base value
O = old base value
P = percentage change

On a spreadsheet, cell values are:

A1   N
B1   O
C1   = SUM((A1-B1)/B1)

▶ Example: Microsoft revenues in 2009 were $58,437 (in millions); in 2008, they were $60,420. Applying the formula:

($58,437 − $60,420) ÷ $60,420 = −3.3%

This change was negative because revenues fell. When revenues rise, the change is positive. However, an analysis of 10 years' change in revenue and profits is not as revealing using this formula because it is based on year-to-year change without regard to the full decade. Microsoft's results for a full decade are summarized in Table 6-3.

The results in the example demonstrate the flaw in using the percentage change for a series of years. The outcome does not accurately summarize the trend. For example, annual changes in the reported net profit range from −18.3% to +50.0% This makes development of a real trend difficult to spot. An alternative is to create a visual summary of the history and track the *trend* over many years.

▶ Example: In the case of the Microsoft revenue trends, a 10-year bar graph is more revealing than percentage change. Figure 6-1 summarizes net profit on a bar graph. This abbreviated but highly visual reflection shows at a glance how the trend has moved over a full decade. In a report that includes a 10-year summary, the actual dollar values probably need to be included, but the chart tells much more.

TABLE 6-3 INCOME STATEMENT

Microsoft Corporation
Annual Percentage Change
10 Years ending 2009

Year	Revenues	% Change	Net Profit	% Change
2000	$22,956	—	$ 9,421	—
2001	25,296	10.2	7,721	− 18.0
2002	28,365	12.1	7,82	91.4
2003	32,187	13.5	9,993	27.6
2004	36,835	14.4	8,168	− 18.3
2005	39,788	8.0	12,254	50.0
2006	44,282	11.3	12,599	2.8
2007	51,122	15.4	14,065	11.6
2008	60,420	18.2	17,681	25.7
2009	58,437	− 3.3	14,569	− 17.6

Source: Standard & Poor's *Stock Reports* and www.microsoft.com/msft/earnings.

FIGURE 6-1 MICROSOFT NET PROFITS

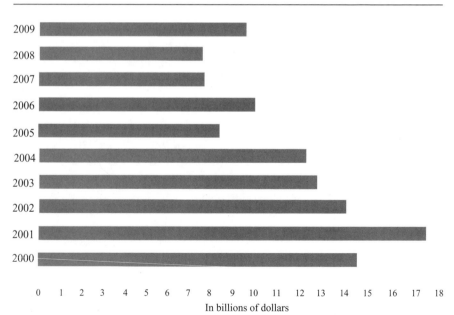

In billions of dollars

COST OF GOODS SOLD RELATIONSHIPS

The relationship between revenue and net profits is the most important ratio on the income statement. However, when you see that the trend is changing over time, a more detailed analysis of changes is required. You need to evaluate the trend in the cost of goods sold as well as the trend in general expenses. The cost of goods sold is distinct and separate from general expenses. These so-called costs are directly attributed to levels of sales volume, whereas expenses occur regardless of increases or decreases in sales.

Costs include:

1. *Merchandise Purchased.* The most significant cost is merchandise. For example, a retail organization purchases merchandise at wholesale, marks it up, and sells it at retail. The cost of merchandise as reported on the income statement has to be adjusted to allow for changes in inventory levels. So if a company allows its inventory level to rise by $100,000 during the year, the true cost of goods *sold* has to be adjusted. To accurately arrive at the cost of merchandise, the formula is:

Cost of Merchandise

$$B + M - E = C$$

where: B = beginning balance of inventory
M = merchandise purchased
E = ending balance of inventory
C = cost of merchandise

▶ Example: A company began the year with $1,855,000 in inventory valued at cost. During the year, $7,400,300 in merchandise is purchased. At the end of the year, the inventory is valued at $1,940,000. The cost of merchandise for the year is:

$1,855,000 + $7,400,300 − $1,940,000 = $7,315,300

The net cost of merchandise is lower than purchases because inventory is higher at the end of the year. If inventory levels are lower at year-end than at the beginning of the year, the cost of merchandise will be higher than the year's purchases.

The formula on a spreadsheet is:

A1   B
A2   M
A3   E
A4   = SUM(A1 + A2-A3)

2. *Direct Labor.* Another important cost factor is direct labor. *Direct* means the payroll costs required to generate product. For example, employees working on an assembly line create the product, so the cost of their labor (e.g., payroll taxes, insurance, and other benefits) is part of direct labor. In comparison, payroll for the accounting department and mail room is properly classified as a general expense. Direct expenses do not directly rise or fall with changes in sales volume.

3. *Transportation Costs.* Another important direct cost involves moving goods from place to place. In any organization that brings product into a site and then moves it out to another site, transportation costs are incurred; and the higher the sales volume, the higher the transportation costs. For example, a company may import unassembled products from overseas, assemble it in its own plant, and then ship it to stores. The cost of bringing products in and then shipping them out are direct costs.

4. *Other Direct Costs.* Depending on the kind of organization, numerous other direct costs are going to be incurred. In a manufacturing environment, direct costs can be very elaborate and may involve detailed breakdowns of plant costs. Under the rules of cost accounting, direct cost analysis and calculation include the assignment of millions of dollars to different product lines and affects how those products are priced.

In manufacturing, inventory is subdivided into categories: raw materials, work in progress, and finished goods. The merchandise and transportation costs may also be assigned to numerous product lines. In companies dealing with a less elaborate series of products, the cost accounting is much easier to calculate. In either case, you need to keep a clear distinction between *direct costs* and *general expenses*. The accurate division of these areas of the income statement is required to properly analyze and spot trends.

As direct costs are studied over a period of time, trends evolve. If the product mix changes, then the relationship between direct costs and revenues changes as well. However, if the mix of products remains unchanged, then in theory the direct cost relationship should remain steady as well. Any changes should be analyzed and explained. For example, direct labor and transportation costs might rise, without a corresponding increase in pricing. That reduces profits as direct costs rise as a percentage of revenue. Companies normally pass on price increases to customers by marking up prices to absorb higher direct costs.

The difference between revenue and direct costs is called *gross profit*. (The formula was shown earlier in the chapter.)

▶ Example: A company reports $13,419,800 in revenue for the year and direct costs of $7,315,300. Gross profit is:

$13,419,800 − $7,315,300 = $6,104,500

In tracking gross profit, it is easier to spot changes in the trend when it is based on a percentage rather than on dollar values.

▶ Example: Here is a five-year summary of revenue, costs, and gross profit using dollar values alone:

Year	Revenue	Direct Costs	Gross Profit
1	$ 8,005,100	$3,901,600	$4,103,500
2	8,616,300	4,478,500	4,137,800
3	10,007,100	5,371,800	4,635,300
4	11,451,200	6,260,200	5,191,000
5	13,419,800	7,515,300	5,904,500

From this dollars-only summary, determining whether the gross profit trend is moving in a positive or negative direction is quite difficult. The desirable outcome is to maintain the relationship at the same level each year, even when revenue is rising. For this you need to calculate the gross margin:

Gross Margin

$G \div R = M$

where: G = gross profit
R = revenue
M = gross margin

On a spreadsheet, gross margin is:

```
A1    G
B1    R
C1    = SUM(A1/B1)
```

▶ Example: Referring to the previous chart, calculating gross margin
results in the following outcome:

Year	Revenue	Direct Costs	Gross Profit	Gross Margin
1	$ 8,005,100	$ 3,901,600	$ 4,103,500	51.3%
2	8,616,300	4,478,500	4,137,800	48.0
3	10,007,100	5,371,800	4,635,300	46.3
4	11,451,200	6,260,200	5,191,000	45.3
5	13,419,800	7,515,300	5,904,500	44.0

The formula applied to the fifth year is:

$5,904,500 ÷ $13,419,800 = 44.0%

This version of the analysis reveals what the numbers alone do not:
The trend shows that gross margin is eroding each year. This affects
profits drastically.

▶ Example: If the fifth year's gross margin had been identical to the first
year's 51.3%, gross profits would have been:

$13,419,800 × 51.3% = $6,884,357

This made a substantial difference in the profitability of the company.
Comparing the above to actual gross profits:

$6,884,357 − $5,904,500 = $979,857

Based on the volume, the change of 7.3% in gross margin cost the
company nearly $1 million in net profits. Assuming that general
expense levels remained fairly steady throughout the five-year
period, this is a significant reduction in potential profits.

This is why the gross margin has to be monitored each year and, when negative trends are spotted, why their causes need to be examined. The change could be a matter of revising product markup for increased costs or needing to improve internal controls due to lower efficiency with higher sales volume.

REVENUE AND PROFITABILITY TRENDS

The gross margin can affect bottom-line profits over time. The erosion in this margin can be caused by many things: rising costs, poor internal controls, or changes in the product mix. However, when it comes to an analysis of expenses, the primary cause for increases is the lack of internal control or follow-through on budgets.

Expenses are not directly related to sales. Some overhead expenses accrue no matter what. So if sales fall from one year to the next, the expense of the long-term lease on the company's offices and warehouses continues at the same rate. If sales rise, the level of administrative salaries and wages should not rise dollar for dollar with sales. With higher volume, you expect such expenses to climb to a degree, but not dollar for dollar. So realistically, many general expenses such as salaries have to rise as sales revenue rises. In time, the company needs more space, more people, and more locations.

The relationship between revenue, costs, and expenses should reflect a tracking between sales and costs and a less reactive rise in general expenses. This relationship is summarized in Figure 6-2. Note how the lines move. You expect costs to follow sales revenue because they are direct, but you also expect expenses to climb only as a result of higher expense levels and not directly in reaction to revenue changes.

Expenses are broken down into two broad classifications.

- *Sales expenses* include the travel expenses of marketing and sales personnel, marketing department telephone and postage expenses, and similar kinds of sales-related items. However, sales expenses rise as sales rise but not at the same rate as costs.
- The better-known *general and administrative expenses (G&A)*—or simply overhead—are fairly fixed. You cannot expect administrative salaries, payroll taxes, rent, telephone, and insurance to change just

FIGURE 6-2 NET PROFIT TRENDS

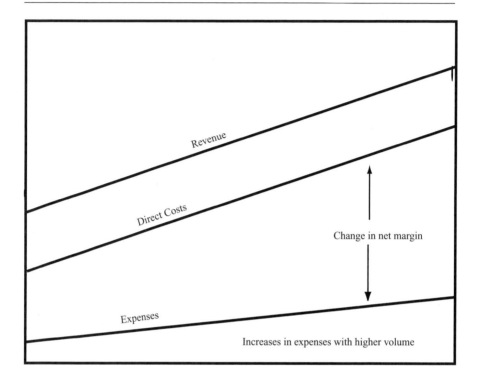

because sales rise and fall. So the fixed nature of G&A is its primary attribute.

Of course, G&A is going to rise as marketing activity increases, but proper internal controls should help to keep such expenses in line. In fact, budgetary control over items such as office supplies, telephone, and postage is where managers can exert the greatest control and protect the bottom-line net profit. One of the greatest dangers in this area is allowing overhead expenses to creep upward when profits are on the rise. Remember, however, that the tracking of net return—like gross margin—occurs on a percentage basis. The ideal trend in net profits contains several attributes:

1. *The dollar amount of expenses does not rise as quickly as revenue or costs.* The purpose of separating direct costs from expenses is to track the changes from year to year. You need to ensure that direct

costs remain steady and do not creep up as sales revenue rises. You also need to implement internal controls so that the percentage of expenses does not move upward more than necessary.

2. *Expenses rise more slowly, in response to increased overhead demands, not in response to heightened sales volume.* Expenses, by definition, should produce greater efficiency per revenue dollar as revenue levels rise. All too often, you see the opposite in times of higher sales. If expenses rise as a percentage of sales, then the net return is also going to decline.

3. *Although the dollar amount of expenses rises, net profit should rise more.* The net return percentage should remain consistent from year to year and should not fall. If it rises, that is a sign of efficiencies gained when revenue levels rise, but the net return should always remain the same as a minimum. Expenses outpacing revenue is a red flag. It means that management is not exerting control over expenses. The negative trend in expenses has an eroding effect on long-term profits. For this reason, organizations that end up going out of business often do so after a period of ever higher sales. They do not control cash flow or expenses. Successful companies know how important it is to hold expense levels in check, *especially* when sales are moving upward rapidly.

CORE EARNINGS

The concept of net income is universally understood, although there are several versions.

- *Net operating income* is the net before other income or expenses and before deducting tax liability.
- *Pretax income* is the combination of operating income and other income or expenses.
- *Net after-tax income* is the so-called net net, or the bottom line after all transactions are calculated.

There is another adjustment, however: *core earnings*. This recalculation of net income is usually based on the net operating income as a starting point. Core earnings is an idea first introduced by the Standard & Poor's Corporation in 2001. The purpose was to make income statements consistent with one another by removing nonoperating income and expenses. The remaining core earnings are the earnings from the company's primary business activity. Profits from pension income, the sale of capital assets, or litigation settlements are deducted from net income to arrive at core earnings. Expenses not directly related to the core activity also have to be deducted from the total.

The core earnings adjustments that a company makes can be considerable. So all income statement ratios and returns can be distorted by the differences between reported and core net income. Some companies have relatively low core earnings adjustments, and others have substantial changes between the two numbers each year.

▶ Example: The differences in net and core earnings for Microsoft (MSFT) and Sears Holding (SHLD) are substantial, with Sears reporting a much higher percentage change between net and core over a five-year period. These companies are in different industries, so profit levels are also vastly different. However, the differences in both dollar amounts and percentages of net profit versus core earnings demonstrate what an important adjustment this is: the greater the change, the greater the impact on all income statement ratios.

A five-year summary for both companies and resulting net return are shown on Table 6-4. Although levels of revenue are approximately the same for each company, the overall net return is significantly different due to the attributes of the two industries. Even so, the core earnings adjustments are more significant on a percentage basis for Sears than for Microsoft. A comparison of the net return and core net return makes this point. Whereas Microsoft's adjustments are consistently within one or two points, Sears had much greater changes, especially in 2005 and 2009.

LOOKING AHEAD

Core earnings can make a big difference in the long-term trend. Using the adjustments helps to ensure that comparisons between two different companies are truly comparable. Yet another concern is the relationship between profitability and cash flow. The most important noncash expense is depreciation, and any calculation of cash-based returns has

TABLE 6-4 NET PROFIT AND CORE EARNINGS

Microsoft (MSFT)

Year	Revenues	Net Profit	Net Return	Core Earnings	Net Core Earnings (%)
2005	$39,788	$12,254	30.8%	$13,107	32.9
2006	44,282	12,599	28.5	13,329	30.1
2007	51,122	14,065	27.5	13,643	26.7
2008	60,420	17,681	29.3	18,873	31.2
2009	58,437	14,569	24.9	14,650	25.1

Sears Holding (SHLD)

Year	Revenues	Net Profit	Net Return	Core Earnings	Net Core Earnings (%)
2005	$19,701	$ 1,106	5.6%	$ 448	2.3
2006	49,124	948	1.9	696	1.4
2007	53,012	1,490	2.8	1,439	2.7
2008	50,703	826	1.6	645	1.3
2009	46,770	53	0.1	− 126	− 0.3

Source: Standard & Poor's Stock Reports for MSFT and SHLD.

to make adjustments to remove depreciation from the net profit. A company that invests in capital assets is allowed to write off a portion of its original cost each year. As this occurs, the asset value is reduced (through a negative asset account called *accumulated depreciation*), and each year's income statement includes an adjustment, made by journal entry, to record depreciation expense. The calculation is mysterious to many, but, upon examination, calculating depreciation is not difficult. The next chapter explains why and how.

CHAPTER 7

Depreciation Calculations

Depreciation is the periodic writing off of capital assets. According to the federal rules:

Depreciation is the annual deduction that allows you to recover the cost or other basis of your business or investment property over a certain number of years. Depreciation starts when you first use the property in your business or for the production of income. It ends when you either take the property out of service, deduct all your depreciable cost or basis, or no longer use the property in your business or for the production of income.[1]

When a business invests in depreciable assets (defined as assets with value exceeding one tax year and used in a trade or business), they are placed on the balance sheet as assets. Each year, a portion is transferred to the income statement as expense with an offsetting entry to an account called accumulated depreciation. By the time the asset is fully depreciated, each year's expense has been recorded properly and the depreciable value of the asset has been reduced to zero (because the sum of accumulated depreciation reduces the asset value).

1. www.irs.gov, instructions for Form 4562.

The accumulated depreciation account is a reduction of the asset. The journal entry to record depreciation is:

Account	Debit	Credit
Depreciation expense	xxx	
Accumulated depreciation		xxx

On the balance sheet, the net value of capital assets is the original basis less accumulated depreciation.

▶ Example: The capital asset section of your company details the classes of capital assets and then deducts accumulated depreciation:

Automobiles and trucks	$ 182,455
Plant machinery	447,313
Real estate	2,450,600
Small tools	84,600
Subtotal	$3,164,968
Less: Accumulated depreciation	994,260
Net long-term assets	$2,170,708

BASIC DEPRECIATION RULES

The rules for calculating and deducting depreciation are set by the Internal Revenue Service. To get an overview of the current rules, go to the website www.irs.gov and download the publication "Depreciation and Amortization" (Publication 4562). A few important rules to keep in mind:

1. *The recovery period is determined by the type of asset.* The IRS has developed a series of specific recovery periods based on the nature of the asset. For example, assets like automobiles and computers are likely to lose value and need replacement much faster than real estate; as a result, the differences in recovery periods are substantial.
2. *The method used to calculate depreciation is determined by the recovery period.* Also prescribed by the IRS are the kinds of depreciation you are allowed to use. For some of the shorter-life assets, you are allowed to accelerate the method so that more write-off takes place at first and less later on when the asset is worth much

less. Longer-term assets, notably real estate, cannot be depreciated on an accelerated basis, but they can be written off only using the straight-line method (in which the same amount is written off each year).

3. *In the case of real estate, only improvements (buildings, etc.) can be depreciated.* Land cannot be depreciated. A special case arises for the depreciation of real estate. You can never depreciate land, which has to be kept on the books indefinitely; it can be removed only when the property is sold.

4. *The basis for depreciation is always the net cost plus improvements, never the current market value.* An oddity in the accounting system is that assets must be depreciated based on actual cost plus improvements, if any. You can never increase the book value of real estate.

▶ Example: A company purchases its land and building for $1.6 million. Ten years later its market value has increased to more than $5 million. Even so, the value reported on the balance sheet declines each year as the building's depreciation is written off. The increased market value is not acknowledged on the balance sheet.

5. *Depreciation begins not when an asset is purchased or paid for, but when it is placed into service.* You might purchase an asset this year but not begin using it until next year. In this situation, you cannot begin to claim the depreciation expense right away. The depreciation begins only in the year the asset is placed into service.

6. *Some elections can be made to alter the method used for depreciation; however, the election has to be applied to all assets in the same class that are placed into service in the same year.* A variety of depreciation-based elections can be made each year. However, you cannot pick and choose. Each asset in the year's recovery period has to be subjected to the same elections.

STRAIGHT-LINE AND DECLINING BALANCE DEPRECIATION

Two kinds of depreciation are used for virtually all calculations: straight-line and declining balance. Straight-line is simply claiming the same amount each year over the life of the asset (its recovery period). Declining balance is a calculation allowing you to claim more depreciation in the early years and less in the later years. Under the IRS-published calculations, for assets that can be accelerated, companies use the declining balance method and then convert to straight-line in later years.

Straight-Line Depreciation

To calculate *straight-line depreciation,* you need to pay attention to the rules governing the first-year levels you are allowed to take (explained later in this chapter). The equation for straight-line depreciation involves a single step:

Annual Straight-Line Depreciation

$B \div Y = D$

where: B = basis
Y = years in the recovery period
D = annual depreciation

On a spreadsheet, the cells are:

A1   B
B1   Y
C1   = SUM(A1/B1)

▶ Example: You purchase an asset for $7,500 and place it into service on January 1 this year. Using the straight-line method and assuming the asset qualifies for a five-year recovery period, the formula is:

$7,500 ÷ 5 = $1,500 per year

To calculate the same level of depreciation but on a monthly basis, the formula is:

Monthly Straight-Line Depreciation

$B \div (Y \times 12) = D$

where: B = basis
Y = years in the recovery period
D = monthly depreciation

On a spreadsheet:

```
A1    B
B1    = SUM(Y*12)
C1    = SUM(A1/B1)
```

Using the same example as before, monthly depreciation is:

$7,500 ÷ (5 × 12) = $125 per month

Declining Balance Depreciation

The method for calculating *declining balance depreciation* is more complex. Under this method, you are allowed to claim more than the straight-line amount per year in the early years and less as time goes on. There are two common methods: 150% and 200%. Under the 150% method, you can deduct 150% of the straight-line depreciation in the first year. Subsequent years are calculated as 150% of the balance remaining. So you begin with the original basis, deduct the first year's depreciation, and then repeat the calculation:

Declining Balance (150%) Depreciation

$[(B - P) ÷ Y] × 150\% = D$

where: B = basis
       P = previous years' accumulated depreciation
       Y = years in the recovery period
       D = annual depreciation

The accumulated depreciation value is necessary to recalculate the basis each year. The basis declines by the total of previously claimed depreciation. On a spreadsheet:

```
A1       B
B1       = SUM((A1/5)*1.5)
C1       = SUM((A1-B1)
A2       = C1
B2, C2   COPY B1 AND C1; PASTE TO B2 AND C2
ROW 3    COPY ALL CELLS, ROW 2; PASTE TO ROW 3
```

▶ Example: You purchase an asset worth $7,500, and you want to apply the 150% declining balance formula. For the first year, this is:

[($7,500 − $0) ÷ 5] × 150% = $2,250

For the second year, the basis is reduced by the amount of depreciation previously claimed:

[($7,500 − $2,250) ÷ 5] × 150% = $1,575

Here is a five-year summary on the spreadsheet:

	A	B	C
1	7,500	2,250	5,250
2	5,250	1,575	3,675
3	3,675	1,103	2,572
4	2,572	772	1,800
5	1,800	540	1,260

For the second type of declining balance, the same formula is used but the multiplier of 1.5 (150%) is replaced with a multiplier of 2 (200%):

Declining Balance (200%) Depreciation

[(B − P) ÷ Y] × 200% = D

where: B = basis
P = previous years' accumulated depreciation
Y = years in the recovery period
D = annual depreciation

The spreadsheet entries:

A1	B
B1	= SUM((A1/5)*2)
C1	= SUM((A1 − B1)
A2	= C1
B2, C2	COPY B1 AND C1; PASTE TO B2 AND C2
ROW 3	COPY ALL CELLS, ROW 2; PASTE TO ROW 3

▶ Example: Using the data from the previous example, the outcome over five years is:

	A	B	C
1	7,500	3,000	4,500
2	4,500	1,800	2,700
3	2,700	1,080	1,620
4	1,620	648	972
5	972	389	583

Because the schedule in these examples calls for a five-year depreciation recovery period, the balance at the end of the fifth year is normally written off in the sixth year. In the tables published by the IRS (shown later in this chapter), declining balance is applied for a specific number of years, and then the schedule reverts to the straight-line method.

CLASS LIVES AND RECOVERY PERIODS

The rules for depreciating assets include a series of class lives, each associated with a recovery period. When assets do not fit into the narrowly defined recovery periods, they are depreciated using the one closest to the reasonable useful life of the asset. The properties classified by recovery period are listed in the IRS instructions for depreciation.

The IRS also specifies a number of conventions for calculating first-year depreciation. Depending on when property is purchased and placed into service, one of the three conventions applies:

1. Half-Year Convention. This system applies to most short-term properties but not to real estate. The assumption under this convention is that no matter when property was actually placed into service, first-year depreciation is one-half of the full-year calculated rate.

▶ Example: Under this convention, if the first year's depreciation is calculated at $2,250, the actual deduction in the first year is $1,125.

Half-Year Convention

$C \div 2 = D$

where: C = calculated full-year depreciation
D = depreciation, first year

On a spreadsheet:

```
A1    C
B1    = (SUM(A1/2)
```

2. *Midquarter Convention.* This method is used in some circumstances and for some kinds of property (see the instructions for depreciation published by the IRS). The assumption is that property is placed into service exactly midway in the quarter. The midpoint in any one quarter is equal to 1.5 months, so the amount allowed varies for each quarter. For example, if you bought equipment during the first quarter, your first-year depreciation will be greater than if you bought it during the fourth quarter, because it would be in service for more time.
Tables summarizing the allowable annual depreciation using the half-year convention and based on 150% declining balance are shown in Table 7-1. A table using 200% declining balance and based on the half-year convention is shown in Table 7-2.

Midquarter Convention

First quarter:

$$C[(1.5 \div 12) \times 7] = D$$

Second quarter:

$$C[(1.5 \div 12) \times 5) = D$$

Third quarter:

$$C[(1.5 \div 12) \times 3) = D$$

Fourth quarter:

$$C[(1.5 \div 12) \times 1] = D$$

where: C = calculated depreciation
D = first-year depreciation

TABLE 7-1 DEPRECIATION: 150% DECLINING BALANCE WITH HALF-YEAR CONVENTION

	Recovery Period (%)					
Year	5-Year	7-Year	10-Year	12-Year	15-Year	20-Year
1	15.00	10.71	7.50	6.25	5.00	3.750
2	25.50	19.13	13.88	11.72	9.50	7.219
3	17.85	15.03	11.79	10.25	8.55	6.677
4	16.66	12.25	10.02	8.97	7.70	6.177
5	16.66	12.25	8.74	7.85	6.93	5.713
6	8.33	12.25	8.74	7.33	6.23	5.285
7		12.25	8.74	7.33	5.90	4.888
8		6.13	8.74	7.33	5.90	4.522
9			8.74	7.33	5.91	4.462
10			8.74	7.33	5.90	4.461
11			4.37	7.32	5.91	4.462
12				7.33	5.90	4.461
13				3.66	5.91	4.462
14					5.90	4.461
15					5.91	4.462
16					2.95	4.461
17						4.462
18						4.461
19						4.462
20						4.461
21						2.231

TABLE 7-2 DEPRECIATION: 200% DECLINING BALANCE WITH HALF-YEAR CONVENTION

	Recovery Period (%)			
Year	3-Year	5-Year	7-Year	10-Year
1	33.33	20.00	14.29	10.00
2	44.45	32.00	24.49	18.00
3	14.81	19.20	17.49	14.40
4	7.41	11.52	12.49	11.52
5		11.52	8.93	9.22
6		5.76	8.92	7.37
7			8.93	6.55
8			4.46	6.55
9				6.56
10				6.55
11				3.28

▶ Example: The calculated depreciation for the first year is $2,250 and property is placed into service during the second quarter. Using the mid-quarter convention, first-year depreciation is:

$$\$2,250[(1.5 \div 12) \times 5] = \$1,406$$

The spreadsheet entries for the midquarter convention are:

```
A1    C
B1      = SUM((1.5/12)*x
C1      = (SUM(A1*B1)
```

▶ Example: In this calculation, the value of x is the factor for each quarter:

First quarter	7
Second quarter	5
Third quarter	3
Fourth quarter	1

3. _Midmonth Convention._ For depreciation on real estate, the assumption is made that property is placed in service halfway through the applicable month. Because there are 24 half-months in each year, the formula is based on calculated halfway points using fractions of 24ths:

Midmonth Convention

$$C(n \div 24) = D$$

where C = calculated depreciation
n = monthly fraction
D = first-year depreciation

The monthly fraction is based on 24 half-months. For example, in the first month of the year, n is valued at 23 using the half-month calculation. Depreciation is going to be equal to 23/24ths of the full-year calculated value. The value of n is equal to:

Month	n	Month	n
1	23	7	11
2	21	8	9
3	19	9	7
4	17	10	5
5	15	11	3
6	13	12	1

The spreadsheet cell entries:

```
A1    C
B1    = SUM(N/24)
C1    = (SUM(A1*B1)
```

▶ Example: You purchased real estate last year and placed it into service during the third month. The calculated depreciation per year is
$8,100. Using the midmonth convention, the formula is:

$8,100 (13 ÷ 24) = $4,387

Residential real estate can be depreciated using only the straight-line
method, and the period for depreciation is 27.5 years. A summary of
each year's percentage of depreciation allowed is summarized in Table
7-3.

Nonresidential real estate is depreciated using the straight-line
method over 39 years. A summary of each year's depreciation is shown
in Table 7-4. Note that a 40th year's depreciation is required due to
partial first-year allowance.

DEPRECIATION CALCULATIONS FOR REAL ESTATE

The depreciable basis of some assets is not always apparent. You may
need to prorate the total basis. Proration—the division of a dollar value
between two or more categories—is commonly used in accounting and
other applications. For example, a company-wide utility expense is likely
to be prorated to each department based on floor space, numbers of
employees, or other logical proration criteria.

In real estate, closing statements prorate property taxes, insurance,

TABLE 7-3 DEPRECIATION: RESIDENTIAL REAL ESTATE WITH MIDMONTH CONVENTION

			The Month in the 1st Recovery Year the Property Is Placed in Service		
Month	Year 1 (%)	Years 2–9 (%)	Years 10, 12, 14, 16, 18, 20, 22, 24, 26 (%)	Years 11, 13, 15, 17, 19, 21, 23, 25, 27 %	Year 28 (%)
1	3.485	3.636	3.637	3.636	1.970
2	3.182	3.636	3.637	3.636	2.273
3	2.879	3.636	3.637	3.636	2.576
4	2.576	3.636	3.637	3.636	2.879
5	2.273	3.636	3.637	3.636	3.182
6	1.970	3.636	3.637	3.636	3.485
7	1.667	3.636	3.636	3.637	3.788
8	1.364	3.636	3.636	3.637	4.091
9	1.061	3.636	3.636	3.637	4.394
10	0.758	3.636	3.636	3.637	4.697
11	0.455	3.636	3.636	3.637	5.000
12	0.152	3.636	3.636	3.637	5.303

interest, and utilities between buyer and seller. The proration is broken down on the basis of days.

▶ Example: A property tax bill is paid twice per year. For this calcula-tion, a year is assumed to consist of 360 days. A transaction closes on the 43rd day of the current 180-day tax period. So the seller is prorated 43/180ths of the bill, and the remaining 137/180ths is assigned to the buyer.

The same treatment of a purchase price has to be used to prorate the cost of property between land (which cannot be depreciated) and improvements (the building, which can be depreciated). However, these values are normally not specified in a property sale; the overall sales price is given, usually without any breakdown. For this reason, you need to calculate the values of land and improvements to calculate depreciation. Three methods can be used to accurately prorate the total basis between land and improvements to determine how much depreciation can be claimed:

TABLE 7-4 DEPRECIATION: NONRESIDENTIAL REAL ESTATE WITH MIDMONTH CONVENTION

	The Month in the 1st Recovery Year the Property Is Placed in Service		
Month	Year 1 (%)	Years 2–39 (%)	Year 40 (%)
1	2.461	2.564	0.107
2	2.247	2.564	0.321
3	2.033	2.564	0.535
4	1.819	2.564	0.749
5	1.605	2.564	0.963
6	1.391	2.564	1.177
7	1.177	2.564	1.391
8	0.963	2.564	1.605
9	0.749	2.564	1.819
10	0.535	2.564	2.033
11	0.321	2.564	2.247
12	0.107	2.564	2.461

1. *Insurance.* The property insurance is based on the estimated replacement value of the improvements. Because this estimate is developed through a study of local costs, it is likely to be an accurate cost estimate for the depreciable portion of the investment.

2. *Appraisal.* The appraisal undertaken for a lender breaks down the estimates of market value for land and improvements, based on recent sales of similar properties in the area.

3. *Assessed Value.* The local taxing authority bases its tax levy on its own estimate of land and improvement value. Although this often is far below market value, the division between the two elements is a reliable basis for dividing the actual cost.

In addition to calculating depreciation (based on time of purchase *and* on valuation of land and improvements), you also need to prorate several expenses based on the time of sale and ownership term for both seller and buyer.

The proration of real estate expenses relies on the number of days before and after the closing date. The property taxes, utilities, rent, and other shared items are split between both sides in calculating proration. The division of real estate expenses is based on the number of days involved. The formula:

Proration

$$V[(a \div) a + b] = P_a$$
$$V[(b \div) a + b] = P_b$$

where: V = value to be prorated
a = proration base factor a
b = proration base factor b
P_a = prorated value of a
P_b = prorated value of b

In this two-part formula, the values a and b add up to the total of the base; and the values of P_a and P_b equal the total of V.
On a spreadsheet:

A1	V
B1	A
C1	B
D1	= SUM(A/(A + B))
E1	= SUM(B/(A + B))
F1	= SUM(A1*D1)
G1	= SUM(A1*E1)

▶ Example of depreciation and other expenses: Your company pur-chases its land and building for $2,650,000. To set up a depreciation schedule, you need to isolate the values of land and improvements. Land cannot be depreciated, so this calculation relies on proration. As of the most recent assessment and tax statement, the assessed value of the property is:

Land	$ 250,000
Improvements	1,665,000
Total	$1,915,000

Using this breakdown as the base, you assign land the value a and improvements the value b. The purchase price of $2,650,000 is the

V you need to break down. Apply the formula and round the outcome to the closest $100:

$2,650,000[$250,000 ÷ ($250,000 + $1,665,000)] = $346,000
$2,650,000[$1,665,000 ÷ ($250,000 + $1,665,000)] = $2,304,000

Now that the values of land and improvements are separated, you are able to apply depreciation correctly. In this example, $2,304,000 can be depreciated. Nonresidential property is depreciated using the straight-line method over 39 years (at $59,076 per year). The annual prorated value of land, or $346,000, remains as an asset on the balance sheet and never changes. It can be removed only when the property is sold.

This proration formula can be used in other applications. The proration of total cost depends on the use of some reliable and applicable base. In the case of accounting decisions, expenses may be divided based on the square footage of a department or the number of employees. For example, when a single value (*V*) has to be divided among multiple people, departments, or recipients, the sum of all base values are added up and expressed as fractions of the total. These are then applied to the single *V* to get the prorated outcomes.

The accuracy of the formula is proven by adding the prorated values and ensuring that they equal the starting value:

Proof of Proration

$$P_a + P_b = V$$

where: P_a = prorated value of a
P_b = prorated value of b
V = value to be prorated

On a spreadsheet program:

A1 P_A
B1 P_B
C1 $= SUM(A1 + B1)$

▶ Example: In the preceding example:

$346,000 + $2,304,000 = $2,650,000

This proves that the formula was applied correctly.

HOME OFFICE DEPRECIATION

Those who work from a home office are allowed to deduct a portion of depreciation and other expenses, and this calculation is another case where proration has to be used. In fact, to calculate depreciation on a qualified home office, two proration steps are necessary. To qualify for a home office deduction, you need to meet a two-part test. First, you have to use the office on a "regular and exclusive" basis. The space cannot double for other purposes. Second, the office must be your principal place of business; in other words, if you conduct business elsewhere, you need to be able to prove that the primary place of business is the home office. Even if you are a manager employed by someone else but you also work at home, you still need to meet these criteria.

For complete information, go to the IRS website at www.irs.gov and download the free Publication 587, "Business Use of Your Home." Deductions are reported on Form 8829, "Expenses for Business Use of Your Home." This can also be downloaded and printed in PDF form from the IRS website.

If you qualify, to calculate the allowable deductions, you first need to determine the prorated space in your home that qualifies.

▶ Example: If you live in a home with total square feet of 3,200 and you qualify for a home office deduction for one room of 350 square feet, the prorated portion of your home is:

350 ÷ 3,200 = 11% (rounded up)

You can deduct 11% of qualified expenses. This deduction includes utilities, homeowners' insurance, insurance, and depreciation. For depreciation, you need to use the proration formula to break down the value of land and improvements, all based not on current value but on your original purchase price.

▶ Example: If you purchased your home for $289,000, you may break down the land and improvements value based on your most recent assessor's statement:

Land	$ 50,000
Improvements	182,000
Total	$232,000

Applying the proration formula:

$289,000[$ 50,000 ÷ ($50,000 + $182,000)] = $ 62,300
$289,000[$182,000 ÷ ($50,000 + $182,000)] = $226,700

This conclusion shows that you can deduct home office expenses based on improvement value of $226,700.

Residential real estate can be depreciated over 27.5 years; in addition, the proration of floor space reveals that the home office represents only 11% of the total. Now you use the formula for the proration of home depreciation:

Home Office Depreciation

$\{[B \times (I \div A)] \div 27.5\} \times (of \div tf) = D$

where: B = basis (purchase price)
I = improvement value (assessed)
A = assessed value, total
of = office square feet
tf = total square feet
D = depreciation allowed

On a spreadsheet:

A1	B
A2	I
A3	A
B1	OF
B2	TF
C1	=SUM((A1*(A2/A3)))

C2   = SUM(C1/27.5)
C3   = SUM((C2*(B1/B2)))

▶ Example:

{[$289,000 × ($182,000 ÷ $232,000)] ÷ 27.5} × (350 ÷ 3,200) = $902.00

This demonstrates that, based on the size of the home office and using the breakdown of the assessed value:

1. A total of 78% of total cost is depreciable ($182,000 ÷ $232,000, applied to the purchase price of $289,000).
2. Only 11% of total floor space can be depreciated as an office in the home.
3. Your qualified home office deduction is $902 per year.

AMORTIZATION

In addition to depreciation, some kinds of expenses are set up as assets and amortized over a period of years. In most instances, amortization is calculated using the straight-line basis. Like depreciation, the annual expense is booked to reflect assigning the cost over a number of years. However, rather than setting up a negative asset account, each year's expense is usually deducted from the asset value on the balance sheet.

Amortization is applied to general expenses that are paid in advance but applied over several years.

▶ Example: Your company paid a 36-month insurance premium in March. This expense applies to a three-year period, so recording the entire expense in the current year is not accurate. Instead the payment is set up as a prepaid asset on the balance sheet. If the total paid is $3,852, the entry is:

Account	Debit	Credit
Prepaid assets	$3,852	
Cash		$3,852

The proper amount to be expensed is equal to 1/36th per month. In the first year, this period covers March through December, or 10 months. So amortization takes place based on this breakdown.

The formula for determining monthly amortization is:

Amortization

$C \div M = A$

where: C = total cost
$\quad\quad M$ = months to amortize
$\quad\quad A$ = amortization per month

On a spreadsheet:

```
A1    C
B1    M
C1     = SUM(A1/B1)
```

▶ Example: Using the information given in the previous example, the current year's expense is 10/36th of the total:

$\$3{,}852 \times (10 \div 36) = \$1{,}070$

The second and third years will each equal 12/36ths (one-third) of the total:

$\$3{,}852 \times (12 \div 36) = \$1{,}284$

The fourth year will recognize the remaining two months of the total:

$\$3{,}852 \times (2 \div 36) = \$214$

At the end of the 36 months, the prepaid asset value will be zero.

A second type of amortization is intended not to properly recognize general expenses, but to write off certain kinds of costs that apply over many years. This is more like the depreciation of capital assets and is applied to tangible costs like research and development or the cost of acquiring a lease. In these instances, the cost is amortized over the applicable period determined by accounting rules.

Amortization can also be applied to *intangible assets,* items shown on the balance sheet but containing no physical value: goodwill, going concern value, brand value, or covenants not to compete. These valuations often are determined at the time of a merger or acquisition and booked according to how a contract is worded. In these instances, the amortization booked as expense each year reduces the value of the intangible asset until it reaches zero.

Looking Ahead

The next chapter moves into the realm of reports. In the body of a report, you can simply list financial information without comment, but that is ineffective. You can also explain the numerical information in a narrative section. Or you can apply ratios and shorthand expressions of the numbers to add powerful and convincing arguments about not only the latest set of financial results, but also how they augment or contradict an established trend.

C H A P T E R   8

Bringing Reports to Life: Powerful Arguments with the Numbers

I f you were not called a "manager," you might be named a "reporter." Managers are expected to report in various ways, to summarize and convey information, to make recommendations, to give early alerts to emerging problems, and to cut costs. The written reports that you prepare and distribute say a lot to others about your professionalism and your ability to communicate.

Even so, some managers struggle with reports because they have not been provided with a few basic skills. These include the ability to *summarize* financial information, explain what it means, and combine it with an informative narrative. The tendency is to simply *include* financial reports, avoid explanation, and provide no narrative supplements. However, whether you are working with a complete set of financial statements, a departmental budget, or a marketing research paper about a new product, you cannot avoid financial data. Once you realize how effective it is to manage the numbers, you will also see that even the dullest topic can spring to life and work as an effective device for conveying your ideas to other managers.

PICKING YOUR REPORT FORMAT

Your first task is to pick the best report format for the topic at hand. No one format is going to work best for every kind of report. As a general rule, remember that, the longer the report is, the less chance it has of even being read. A three-page summary is much more effective than a highly detailed 80-page analysis.

Here are a few ways to keep your report short:

1. *Provide a summary only, but have supporting documents ready.* Assume that anyone receiving your report is going to give it only a glance. Whether produced online or in hard copy, the report is rarely going to be read cover to cover. So a two- or three-page report that gives your conclusions and highlights is far more effective than a longer version. Readers who want to see the supporting documentation can be referred to a backup report or online link. However, the majority of readers will accept your conclusions without asking for proof. Having the supporting documents ready is important, but just as important is providing them only on request.

2. *Organize the report assuming that your audience will read only the first paragraph.* Put your most important point on the first page. Be clear, concise, and brief. Many people, even those who need the information, will read only the first paragraph. So what one thing do you need readers to know? That one thing has to go right at the start of the report. A second suggestion is to include your conclusion in the title of the report. A title like "Keys to a 10% Growth in Market Share" is much more interesting than "Third-Quarter Marketing Forecast."

3. *Never include pages full of numbers in the body of the report. Charts and graphs say much more.* As important as the dollar values and statistics are, they are boring. The more numerical information you include in your report, the less likely it is that people will read it and, more to the point, the less likely they are to comprehend it. Remember, your report's purpose is to reveal information and to

express ideas, not to fill pages with columns and rows of numbers. Refer readers to an appendix if they want the details or to an online site where your spreadsheets are included with all the details and explanations. In the report itself, leave out the details and focus on the information you need your reader to hear.

Base the formatting of a report on these few guidelines. The shorter the report, the better.

Next, determine whether the report should be organized to provide in-depth narratives or a very brief look at (a) a conclusion, (b) recommendations, and (c) details. In other words, the shaping of the report is dictated by its intention.

▶ Examples:

- If your report is a bid for an engineering project, you need to provide statistical information and explain how you will approach the job. You are competing with others who are also bidding on the same job.
- If your report is providing a cost-reduction recommendation, you need to explain the problem and then document your solution.
- If your report addresses methods for increasing market share for your products, you need an analysis of customers, the competition, and methods for achieving the market expansion goals.

Even so, the same basic rules apply. Keep the report as short as possible, avoid massive numerical sections, and prioritize. You can probably think of dozens of reports you might be asked to prepare or that you will need to review from other managers or employees. If the same format is applied in each case, the effectiveness is lost. Even if most people are using a similar format, be ready to think creatively. The key to selecting the right presentation is based on how you want to convey the essential information in your report.

The report may consist of narrative or financial sections or a combination of both. Even if you do not want to place the details elsewhere, you can assign financial details to an appendix and then explain them in summarized form. Using graphics, ratios, and narratives, you should be able to create a user-friendly reporting format that works best in each situation.

Reports tend to fall into two classifications. The recurring format is in the minority, and the more common one-time report is the rule.

NARRATIVE SECTIONS

A report can consist primarily of narrative sections. By itself, a long narrative is uninteresting and difficult to read, especially for a dry topic. However, a few short but informative departures vastly improve the narrative. Such departures can take the form of:

1. *Sidebars.* A sidebar is a related thought and a form of emphasis that is set aside from the narrative and boxed off in some way. This is used freely in magazine articles. Also termed a *call-out*, the sidebar breaks up the discussion and brings your primary point to the reader's attention. The use of sidebars should be limited, but, for example, if your report needs to get across three major ideas, use sidebars. Even a casual glance at your report will highlight the main ideas.

2. *Tables.* It is very difficult to read a report containing a lengthy explanation of the numbers. A table can summarize a numerical portion of the report, if it must be included.

▶ Example: Compare the following two paragraphs:

Approach 1

During the quarter, several important improvements occurred in the marketing activity of the branch. The western division moved sales volume from $425,000 up to $519,000 over the prior quarter, a growth rate of 22.1%. The southern division saw growth from $318,000 in sales to $341,000, an improvement over the prior quarter of 7.2%. The central division grew in sales volume from $543,000 to $602,000, or 10.9%. The northern division, the newest expansion in the branch, grew from $127,000 to $172,000, an improvement of 35.4%. Only the eastern division had a decline, changing from the prior quarter's total of $288,000 to current quarter of $251,000, a decline of 14.7%.

Approach 2

Four out of five divisions in the branch experienced growth during the
quarter:

Division	Prior	Current	Change (%)
Western	$425,000	$519,000	22.1
Southern	318,000	341,000	7.2
Central	543,000	602,000	10.9
Northern	127,000	172,000	35.4
Eastern	288,000	251,000	− 14.7

The decline is attributed in part to the loss of our divisional manager
during the quarter. The decline is not expected to continue.

The second approach summarizes the financial information in a separate table and also adds a brief explanation for the disappointing
results in one out of five divisions. The second approach is preferable
because it is easier to digest and to comprehend.

3. *Charts and Graphs.* Using charts and graphs is an excellent way
to liven up a report. Financial information is difficult for people to
understand in context, and it is easier to grasp when summarized visually.

▶ Example: Figure 8-1 shows the same data as in the previous example
but in a bar graph—a vast improvement over even the table. The
graph not only shows the quarter-to-quarter change but also provides
a visual comparison between divisions. This method of conveying
information is far superior to the narrative paragraph and to the table.

4. *Footnotes.* Using footnotes livens up a report, while enabling you
to place secondary thoughts apart from the text. Footnoting is also a
subtle form of emphasis that breaks up an otherwise monotonous report.

▶ Example: Returning to the previous example, the discussion of sales
volume by branch division could be set up in the following way:

Four out of five divisions in the branch experienced growth during the
quarter, summarized below:

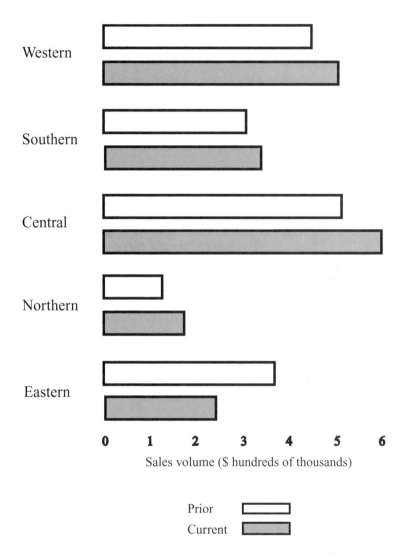

The decline in the Eastern Division is not expected to continue.[1]

This use of a footnote enables you to elaborate on an important point, but without breaking up the rhythm of the narrative. Footnotes can also be used for nonessential but interesting facts that add to the tone of your report.

1. The eastern divisional manager left the organization during the quarter, creating temporary turmoil and a leadership gap. We have since replaced him and current trends are returning to prior levels.

FIGURE 8-1 VOLUME OF SALES BY DIVISION, QUARTERLY COMPARISON

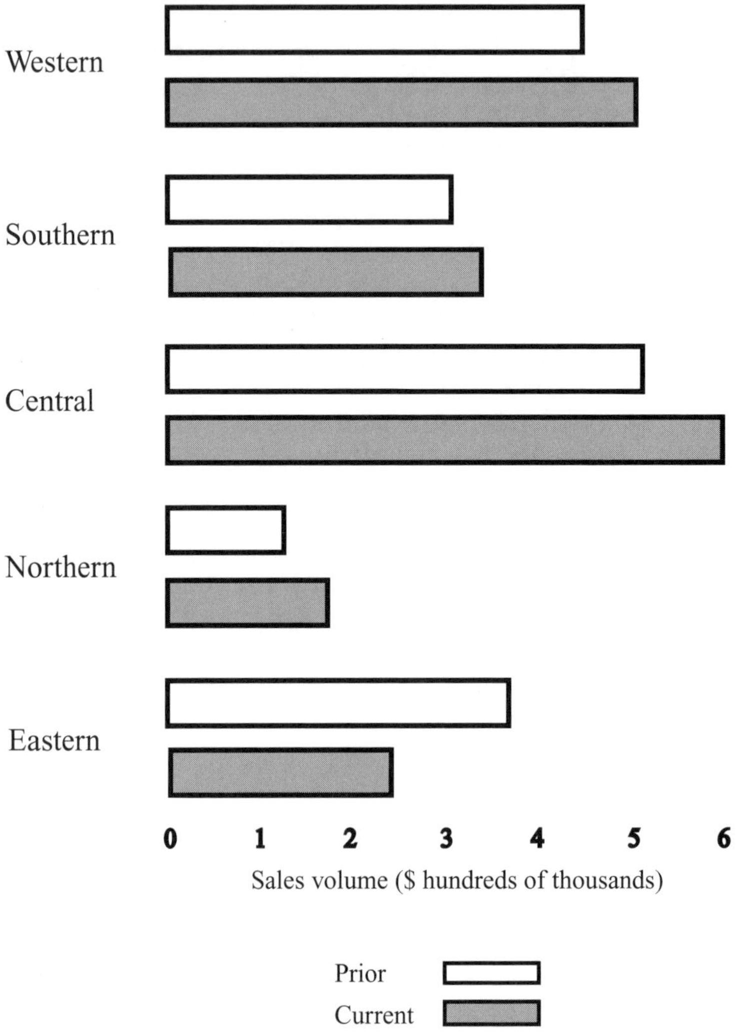

Sales volume ($ hundreds of thousands)

Prior

Current

5. *Narrative forms of emphasis.* The easiest and most apparent form of emphasis in a report is typographic emphasis. It is easily overused, however, and should be avoided. Even a very short paragraph loses its impact if overly emphasized.

▶ **Example: Consider this short paragraph:**

Marketing volume has been exceptionally strong this quarter due to the recent acquisition of our only major competitor. However, we also expect a finite growth curve as we saturate a limited customer base.

This statement is extremely important. Wanting to ensure that its importance is appreciated, a report writer might be tempted to overuse typographic emphasis.

▶ **Examples:**

Italicizing

Marketing volume has been exceptionally strong this quarter due to the recent acquisition of our only major competitor. However, we also expect a finite growth curve as we saturate a limited customer base.

Underlining

Marketing volume has been exceptionally strong this quarter due to the recent acquisition of our only major competitor. However, we also expect a finite growth curve as we saturate a limited customer base.

Boldface

Marketing volume has been exceptionally strong this quarter due to the recent acquisition of our only major competitor. However, we also expect a finite growth curve as we saturate a limited customer base.

Capitalizing

MARKETING VOLUME HAS BEEN EXCEPTIONALLY STRONG THIS QUARTER DUE TO THE RECENT ACQUISITION OF OUR ONLY MAJOR COMPETITOR. HOWEVER, WE ALSO EXPECT A FINITE GROWTH CURVE AS WE SATURATE A LIMITED CUS-TOMER BASE.

Larger Font

Marketing volume has been exceptionally strong this quarter due to the recent acquisition of our only major competitor. However, we also expect a finite growth curve as we saturate a limited customer base.

All these forms of emphasis are obnoxious and tedious because they are used in excess. With the nearly universal use of easy-to-use word processing programs, all these forms of emphasis (as well as others, such as text highlighting or formatting changes) or combined forms of emphasis (such as italics, underlines, and all-caps used together) are even more ineffective. Even bad habits like capitalizing every word in a sentence or placing quotation marks around nonquote items are merely distracting.

▶ **Example:**

"Marketing Volume" Has Been Exceptionally Strong This Quarter Due To The Recent Acquisition Of Our Only "Major Competitor." However, We Also Expect A "Finite" Growth Curve As We Saturate A "Limited" Customer Base.

The distracting formatting of this paragraph makes the message difficult to comprehend. The use of capitals and quotation marks adds nothing; in fact, it makes the message less clear.

FINANCIAL SECTIONS

Many reports contain sections of narrative and financial material. Whether financial reports are provided in an appendix or mixed in with narrative explanations, the use of a large volume of numbers is a problem. If the rows and columns of financial information are not presented interestingly, many readers are going to skip over them or fail to grasp their importance. Report preparers miss a great opportunity to bring the numbers to life by not considering how to design the report to maximize its effectiveness.

When you have to prepare a report heavily loaded with financial data, you face a challenge. Many reports contain a great deal of financial reporting, but the most effective reports are readable, visual, and short. Even when the financial sections are lengthy, there are good solutions:

1. *Use an appendix.* Keep the body of your report to as few pages as possible. Put supporting documentation in an appendix so that readers can refer to it without extra steps.
2. *Creates links to separated financial data.* Place financial supporting data in a separate online link, and provide the link within the report at spots where financial data are referenced.
3. *Summarize the key items but exclude the details.* Highlight your important conclusions based on the financial data, but don't automatically assume that your readers want to see the details.
4. *Offer to provide backup on request, but exclude the financial details from the report.* Most people appreciate a short report, and they are more likely to read a short one. For those wanting all of the details, invite requests. You probably will not get many people asking for the financial backup, but offer to provide it.
5. *Break down full-page financial reports into smaller sections.* For example, if part of your report includes a complete set of financial statements, present the assets on a half-page within a narrative section, and then present liabilities and net worth later. You can also break down revenues/costs/gross profit and expenses/net profit into different sections. A widespread assumption is that financial reports must be provided intact, but doing so makes little sense.

The important point is that your reports should be digestible, and a lot of numbers are difficult to manage all at once. Break them up. The same logic applies to numbers in any form: marketing reports or forecasts, budgets, cost breakdowns, manufacturing estimates. All of these are more effectively reported in sections.

A SMART GUIDELINE

Any time your report includes a full page of numerical information, question how it can be broken down into smaller pieces. No one likes poring over a page full of rows and columns of numbers. You will do better with a limited presentation, the numbers represented in graphs or explained with ratios, and key information emphasized and explained.

Any of these methods or any combinations of them make your reports more efficient.

Other methods enable you to mathematically summarize numbers:

1. *Use percentages instead of dollar values for broad statements.* Avoid the use of dollar values in narrative sections. They are difficult to comprehend, especially in comparative form. You can be far more effective using percentage-of-change statements.

▶ Example: "The revenue total rose from $516,078 to $602,994." This change and its significance are not easy to grasp. In comparison, most people can readily understand the expression, "Revenues rose during the quarter by 17%." [Remember the formula for percentage of change: ($602,994 − $516,078) ÷ $516,078 = 17%.]

Percentages bring the numbers to life when used in comparison form.

▶ Example: If revenues rose $516,078 to $602,994, what if costs and expenses rose from $438,540 to $485,916? What does this mean? You can create a dramatic contrast with the statement: "While revenues rose in the quarter by 17%, costs and expenses rose only 11%. This explains the dramatic increase in net operating profit from 15% last quarter to 19% this quarter." (Net is calculated by subtracting costs and expenses from revenues: $516,078 − $438,540 = $77,538 and $602,994 − $485,916 = $117,078. Net return is calculated by dividing net profit by revenues: $77,538 ÷ $516,078 = 15% and $117,078 ÷ $602,994 = 19%.)

2. *Describe change in terms of the "number of times" greater or smaller rather than listing the dollar amounts.* Avoid dollar values in narrative sections whenever possible.

▶ Example: Given the information from the previous example, a better presentation is, "Revenues increased by 1.17 times over the past quarter" ($602,994 ÷ $516,078). Or describe net profit changes as,

"Net operating profits surpassed the previous quarter by 1.51 times"
($117,078 ÷ $77,538).

3. *Express the important features of numerical trends in narrative-based ratio expressions.* Another version of the nondollar expression of results is the use of ratio-type expressions in place of dollar values or percentages.

▶ Example: Rather than stating that revenues this quarter are 1.17 times higher, the ratio version is, "The change in revenues was 1.17 to 1 over the prior quarter." Although this phrasing is the same as a percentage increase, it is easier to digest than percentages.

Many readers are going to be uncomfortable with any form of math, including percentages, but they can easily understand and appreciate what "1.17 to 1" means. It's the same thing, but expressed in a less intimidating way.

COMBINING NARRATIVE AND FINANCIAL CONTENT

In any report where you combine narrative and financial information, you face a dilemma. You want to reduce exposure to the numerical information, but you often are required to include and disclose the full range of results. This is when an appendix is a good idea. Unfortunately, separating the financial data from the discussion is not always effective. This is where two additional reporting tools are effective: annotation and highlighting.

Annotation

Annotation is an effective highlighting tool for bringing numbers to life, and for combining narrative and financial sections. If the inclusion of financial information is unavoidable, you can use annotation to explain the numbers.

▶ Example: Consider the following summarized profit and loss statement:

Revenue	$14,862,300
Cost of goods sold	− 7,992,500
Gross profit	$ 6,869,800
General expenses	− 4,481,500
Net operating profit	$ 2,388,300
Other income and expense	107,900
Net pretax profit	$ 2,496,200
Less: Liability for taxes	− 743,900
Net after-tax profit	$ 1,752,300

By itself, this summary may be interesting, but it does not reveal the significance of the changes in trends. You can use annotation to make this summary far more interesting. Figure 8-2 shows how this is accomplished.

Highlighting

When you have to combine narrative and financial information, it can be made interesting. You can highlight specific information by means of many devices, including the limited use of boldface, italics, larger fonts, underlining, and call-outs.

FIGURE 8-2 ANNOTATED FINANCIAL DATA

Revenue	$14,862,300	19% Increase over last quarter
Cost of goods sold	− 7,992,500	
Gross profit	$ 6,869,800	46.2% Gross profit
General expenses	− 4,481,500	
Net operating profit	$ 2,388,300	
Other income and expense	107,900	16.1% versus only 11.5% last quarter
Net pretax profit	$ 2,496,200	
Less: Liability for taxes	− 743,900	
Net after-tax profit	$ 1,752,300	Highest net on record

▶ Example: Use a call-out to provide details of the cost of goods sold or to provide the comments shown in the annotated form in Figure 8-2. Too many reports simply list the data.

▶ Example: The following paragraph is a fairly typical reporting of financial data:

Quarterly revenues were $14,862,300, 19% higher than last quarter. Cost of goods sold was $7,992,500 and gross profit was $6,869,800, or 46.2% gross margin. General expenses were $4,481,500, for a net operating profit of $2,388,300, or 16.1% (compared to only 11.5% last quarter). Other income was $107,900 and pretax profit was $2,496,200. After deducting tax liabilities of $743,900, the net after-tax profit was $1,752,300, the highest net profit on record.

The problem with a narrative summary is that it provides obvious information (such as the cost of goods sold *and* gross profit) but does not comment on its significance. This report would be far more interesting with either annotation or highlighting in some form.

▶ Example: Consider a revised paragraph:

This was a quarter of new records. Quarterly revenues 19% higher than last quarter and gross margin remained steady at 46.2%. Internal controls produced an impressive 16.1% net operating profit, 4.6% higher than last quarter. Net after-tax profit was $1,752,300, the highest net profit on record. (Details provided on next page.)

The next page then contains the relatively dry numerical summary, preferably with annotated commentary.

This shortened paragraph is far more effective because it explains what is significant in the latest report, and it does so without listing any dollar values. The abbreviated presentation is acceptable because the financial summary is shown on the following page, along with the emphasis where attention belongs. A comparison between both versions of this paragraph demonstrates how a dull, monotonous report can be livened up and made interesting.

GRAPHICS IN REPORTS

Including graphs in your reports makes a tremendous amount of difference. In the past, before spreadsheet-based graphics were possible, report preparers had to rely on a company's art department or outside graphics companies to prepare charts. Preparing charts was time-consuming and expensive, and as a consequence most internal reports lacked graphics or included only crudely drawn approximations.

In constructing graphs using the easy facilities provided in word processing or spreadsheet programs, remember a few guidelines:

1. *Make sure the graphic is used only for important information.* Avoid the temptation to graphically illustrate everything, even the most obvious data. Reserve graphic treatment to summarize the numbers, to visually show a trend, or to compare two or more trends.
2. *Select the most appropriate graph.*

- A *single bar chart* is applicable to a single trend over time. In this type, either a trend or a comparative outcome is reported. For example, the portion of revenues assigned to expenses could be shown gradually growing over time on a single bar chart. Or a single period's breakdown of major expense categories could be reported, showing where the company is spending money.
- A *double bar chart* is the best for showing two or more factors for several groups. In Figure 8-1, this was used to show sales comparisons for several divisions. The graph provided not only the change within each division, but a visual comparison between divisions as well.
- A *line graph* is useful for tracking a trend over many months or years.
- Finally, a *pie chart* shows a circular summary of information; for example, where does the average dollar of revenue go each year? The pie chart breaks down this information into degrees of the circle. The calculation requires two separate steps: percentage of the total and the breakdown into degrees. Any value with several parts can be broken down into percentages of the total, always adding up to 100%. Then those percentages are multiplied by 360 to arrive at the degrees of the circle. For example, 15% is always equal to 54 degrees (15% $\times$ 360 = 54°).

Percentage of the Total

$V \div T = P$

where: V = value
T = total
P = percentage of the total

On a spreadsheet:

A1   T
COPY A1
PASTE TO A2, A3, ETC.
B1   V(1)
B2   V(2)
B3   V(3)
B4   V(4)
C1 $= \text{SUM}(\text{B}1/\text{A}1)$
COPY C1
PASTE TO C2, C3, ETC.

▶ Example: Total revenue is known to be $14,862,300. This consists of the cost of goods sold, general expenses less other income, liability for taxes, and net after-tax profit. Each of these represents a percentage of the total:

Cost of goods sold	7,992,500 ÷ 14,862,300 = 53.8%
General expenses and other income	4,373,600 ÷ 14,862,300 = 29.4
Liability for taxes	743,900 ÷ 14,862,300 = 5.0
Net after-tax profit	1,752,300 ÷ 14,862,300 = 11.8
Total	100.0%

Next, the breakdown is applied to calculate degrees of the circle:

Degrees of a Circle

$P \times 360 = D$

where: P = percentage of the total
D = degrees

On a spreadsheet:

A1   P
B1   = SUM(A1*360)

▶ Example: You are preparing a pie chart to show how each dollar of revenue is spent during the quarter, based on the latest income statement. Total revenue was $14,862,300. The *P* values are:

Cost of goods sold	53.8%
General expenses and other income	29.4
Liability for taxes	5.0
Net after-tax profit	11.8
Total	100.0%

Applying the formula, first convert the percentages to decimal form and then multiply:

Cost of goods sold	0.538 × 360 = 194
General expenses and other income	0.294 × 360 = 106
Liability for taxes	0.050 × 360 = 18
Net after-tax profit	0.118 × 360 = 42
Total	360 degrees

After you calculate the degrees, the values are converted to the pie-chart-formatting feature, and the pie chart is produced. Figure 8-3 shows the outcome.

This type of chart is particularly dramatic because it shows how each dollar of revenue is applied. Although the numbers by themselves and even the trends in the numbers represent meaningful information, nothing compares to a visual summary.

LOOKING AHEAD

The next chapter focuses on a particular type of report that every manager contends with and that most managers dread: the budget. The chapter demonstrates how you can thoroughly document assumptions to turn a budget burden into an effective management tool.

FIGURE 8-3 PIE CHART FOR FINANCIAL REPORT

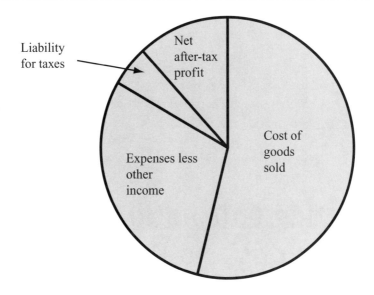

C H A P T E R   9

Budgeting Calculations: Assumptions and Prorations

B udgets have been described as a list of priorities and as "political" documents.[1] They are political in the sense that, in the course of setting priorities in an organization, the individual who has authority to prepare and approve budgets determines where money is going to be spent, which segments or departments will be expanded or allowed to hire employees, and which projects will rise to the top of the priority list.

With this reality in mind, delegating the budgeting process and its approval to others makes little sense. Every manager has a vested interest in setting goals for the coming year, overseeing a budget designed to meet those goals, and establishing internal controls to ensure that expenses do not outpace revenue and exceed appropriately established limits.

Whether you prepare a budget directly or supervise others, or even if your budget is prepared outside your area of control and presented to

1. Edward K. Hamilton, *New York Times*, February 9, 1971: "A budget is a statement of priorities, and there's no more political document."

you for review, remember a few very key considerations when going through the budgeting process:

1. *Every budget should be based on sensible assumptions.* The assumptions are the underlying justifications for all budget items. Simply increasing last year's budget by 5% without clarifying assumptions is ineffective. That process—which is the way most budgets are prepared—does not establish any spending controls. It only makes past spending excesses permanent.
2. *Preparing a budget for more than one fiscal year makes no sense.* The purpose of the budget is to set goals for net profits, based on controlling expense levels. However, because the environment is constantly changing, even a full-year budget cannot be expected to accurately predict the future.
3. *Six-month revisions are essential, but they have to be based on reality.* Assumptions need to be updated. If they are not, the revised budgets simply perpetuate the mistakes made in the original budget. Rather, a revision should update logical assumptions to keep the budgeting process effective and valuable.
4. *The true purpose of budgeting is to monitor progress.* The budget should serve as a financial expression of future goals, based on underlying assumptions. The budget therefore details portions of a larger goal. The purpose is not to ensure that actual expenses will fall under budget in each case, but to provide a means to check progress, recognize internal control problems, and fix those problems as they arise.
5. *Even with the proper use of a budget, it remains a political document.* Even if you properly prepare and use a budget, you cannot get around the fact that it is a political statement of priorities. Competition within an organization for a larger budget and for more status and power defines how budgets are prepared and revised. Ultimately, budgets are also used to identify success and failure in an organization.

Documenting Your Assumptions

When you review a budget, do you just check the variances? These important outcomes, the differences between the budgeted and the actual totals, are only one of the factors you need to keep in mind. An equally crucial piece of information is the underlying assumption. For example, do you assume that the expense level will be the same as last year's? Are you factoring in any increases? Are you using the most applicable base?

Although variances are important, so are the assumptions. Here are some typical assumption bases you need to use in preparing a budget (or that you should expect to find when reviewing budgets prepared by someone else):

1. *Relationship to revenue growth.* Some general expenses are going to change based on known or planned changes in the volume of sales.

   ▶ Example: If your company is acquiring another, you are going to increase your floor space, number of employees, and internal expenses (shipping, telephone, office supplies, telephone, utilities). Even though expenses are not direct, as are costs, the overall level of expenses is going to rise or fall based on changes in revenue.

2. *Expenses varying by number of employees.* One way to reliably budget many kinds of expenses is by the number of employees.

   ▶ Example: You can analyze your office supply expenses by expense per person. To check this, compare several years' worth of supply and employee levels. The same rule may apply to printing, delivery, telephone, and several other administrative expenses.

3. *Marketing expenses such as auto and travel.* Sales and marketing expenses often are listed separately from general and administrative expenses because there is a strong correlation between the volume of sales and marketing expenses. If your company is initiating a new product line, creating new incentives for salespeople, expanding a supply chain, and making other changes in how products or services are delivered, then marketing expenses have to be adjusted realistically at the same time.

4. *Inflation and economic factors.* Most often overlooked in the budget are the unavoidable effects of inflation and other economic changes.

▶ Examples:

- The price of gasoline affects auto and sales expenses.
- Utility rate increases directly affect your expense totals.
- If you deal overseas, foreign currency exchange fluctuations will have an immediate effect on virtually every line of your income statement.

5. *Efficiency from consolidation and internal controls.* If you have put new internal controls in place, you naturally expect to generate savings, which should be reflected in the budget, where you monitor the expense. If you have consolidated departments or segments, you would also expect to realize efficiency and lowered expenses. These changes have to be folded into your budget assumptions.

6. *Changes in internal procedures, including improved efficiency.* Any internal change in procedures will have an impact, hopefully a reduction in expenses. This should be allowed for in the budget assumptions.

▶ Example: If you have been relying on outside services for expenses such as printing or payroll, and this year you are bringing these services in-house, you will have immediate changes in expense levels.

In preparing a budget, fully document the detailed expense categories by assumption base, and then break them down by month. To what extent this process is a so-called best guess depends on the strength of your information. This is where math comes into the picture. Most expense categories can be budgeted on the basis of known information, historical trends, or revenue forecasts. However, some expenses simply cannot be based on solid assumptions. If you have no sensible assumption for budgeting an expense, how do you proceed?

The answer is that you have to rely on math to create a best-guess budget.

▶ Example: Telephone expenses have been rising over the past year, but you cannot identify a base for building an assumption. Lacking any reliable assumption base, you turn to the *trend* to create your budget. During the past year, this expense was booked in the following amounts for your department:

January	$1,221	July	$1,777
February	1,242	August	1,804
March	1,231	September	1,816
April	1,282	October	1,990
May	1,336	November	1,910
June	1,545	December	1,915

The general trend over the course of the year was upward. However, there is no recognizable seasonal or cyclical change to blame. The number of employees has remained unchanged, and no marketing activity is generated in your department, so changes in personnel, revenue, or marketing cannot be blamed for this increase. Telephone rates did increase to a degree, but the increases cannot account for the significant change experienced by your department. So one conclusion might be that the telephone expense is not being properly controlled internally. Also, initial research indicates that another 5% change in billing rates is going to occur during the first quarter, so this has to be built into the budget too. However, you also believe that some abuses have occurred during the year, accounting for the growth in rates from an average of about $1,250 per month up to more than $1,900, an increase of over 50%.

ADDRESSING THE EXPENSE ISSUES

The budget should serve as a means for monitoring the solutions you put into place and for making judgments about their effectiveness. This requires taking some chances. If your internal controls are not effective or if you are mistaken about how effectively you can keep expenses low, you will experience unfavorable variances. Some managers allow budgets to be set too high just to avoid variances, whereas others view unfavorable variances as an opportunity to identify and fix problems.

You take the action to improve internal procedures.

▶ Examples:

• Announce a new monitoring process and remind employees that the personal use of telephones is a violation of company policy.

- Establish a manual phone log to be used for any and all long-distance use of the phone.
- Improve internal procedures for identifying long-distance calls by individual telephone.

Such procedures should be manageable because no marketing activity comes from the department. The only long-distance calls should be made to branch offices or to the home office. Modern telephone systems make fixed-fee telephone usage possible, but this is considered too expensive for a nonmarketing department.

Your budgeting assumptions should be based on valid information, such as the history of telephone expenses and your control measures. As a budgeting philosophy, budget levels can be calculated arbitrarily or simply as an expansion of the previous year's actual expenses. However, either approach results in ever higher budgets and no controls. If the previous year's expenses were not controlled and then are used as the basis for the new budget, then the method is flawed. The budget is valuable as a control mechanism only if the underlying assumptions make sense and provide you with the ability to control expense levels based on rational, realistic, and identifiable criteria.

▶ Example: Your budgeting of telephone expenses would include the following:

- A reasonable telephone expense is $1,200 per month at the beginning of the year, with a 5% increase to $1,260 beginning in March.
- The internal controls announced and put into place are expected to have an immediate effect and reduce monthly charges.
- A quarterly allowance of $150 will be added to the beginning of the first month in the quarter for long-distance usage based on documented phone log entries.

To properly document your budget for the year, include all such components in the monthly budget.

► Example:

Month	Base Expense	Rate Increase	Long Distance	Total
January	$ 1,200		$150	$1,350
February	1,200			1,200
March	1,200	$ 60		1,260
April	1,200	60	150	1,410
May	1,200	60		1,260
June	1,200	60		1,260
July	1,200	60	150	1,410
August	1,200	60		1,260
September	1,200	60		1,260
October	1,200	60	150	1,410
November	1,200	60		1,260
December	1,200	60		1,260
Total	$14,400	600	$ 600	$15,600

Although you cannot expect budget line items—in this case, telephone expenses—to conform exactly to this budget, you have the assumption base as a starting point. You can monitor each month's actual expenses against the budget and identify where problems continue to occur. If the budget turns out to be legitimately inaccurate, having a well-documented assumption base for your budget allows you to identify the reasons and to fix the budget at a six-month revision. Without the assumption base, you simply have no way to know whether expenses are too high.

This budget also allows you to monitor the success of your new internal procedures. If the very high monthly usage rate suddenly falls back to the base rate of $1,200 per month, that tells you that past abuse of the system has stopped due to the announcement of new monitoring.

These budget assumptions are defendable because they completely document how you arrived at the budget. Another common method—taking the past year's total expense and dividing it by 12 to arrive at a monthly budget—is much less effective. When expenses run over the month's budget, how do you explain the variance? The strength and detail of the assumption base give you the means to explain variances, and when you lack an assumption base you cannot possibly defend or explain the budget.

The essential purpose in budgeting is to create a mathematically detailed and itemized rationale for the monthly expense total. This total is then used to compare budgeted to actual figures and to identify areas where:

- Problems exist and require fixing.
- The budget was inadequate.
- Or the realistic level of expense was not anticipated when the budget was prepared.

Any of these outcomes is acceptable because it improves information and gives you what you need to improve the budgeting process. The only undesirable outcome is when assumptions are not documented well enough to provide explanations for shortfalls.

Prorating Expense Estimates

A process that comes up often in budgeting is *proration*, the division of a single item among many different departments or segments. The formula for proration (introduced in an earlier chapter) can be used to calculate the proration of expenses during the budget process.

▶ Example: Your company is budgeting by department and the accounting department's manager is creating a basis for the proration of several expenses. Among these are facilities rent, utilities, and local taxes.

The assignment of such expenses to each department is a debatable practice. Some organizations undergo an extensive, often arbitrary, process of assigning such expenses, leaving no opportunity for a department to control or reduce the expense. So why prorate the budget? It makes more sense to create a corporate budget shell for expenses that cannot be prorated.

However, whenever the decision to prorate has been made, developing a logical method is important.

▶ Example: In the cases of both rent and utilities, the decision was made to prorate monthly expenses on the basis of the square feet occupied by each department. Some square footage in the building cannot be assigned—hallways, meeting rooms, and utility areas. These are ignored; only the square footage of each department is added up. Last year, the rent expense was $4,400 per month and utilities averaged $750. The square footage was calculated as:

Department A	$1,100
Department B	950
Department C	2,235
Department D	1,570
Total	$5,855

These totals were assigned a percentage of the total, and they are to be assigned to rent and utilities each month:

Department A	1,100 ÷ 5,855 = 19%
Department B	950 ÷ 5,855 = 16
Department C	2,235 ÷ 5,855 = 38
Department D	1,570 ÷ 5,855 = 27
Total	100%

The decision to alter monthly levels like these should depend on historical changes.

▶ Example: Rents may be increased annually based on changes in local property tax assessments or upon the expiration-and-renewal dates of the lease. Utility costs should be carefully analyzed to approximate seasonal increases or decreases based on weather.

Using proration for company-wide expenses is problematical as a budgeting method. A basic rule worth observing is that a department should have the full capability to control every item in its budget. Failing this aim, the budget remains a strictly political or bureaucratic tool with no lasting value. A manager might be criticized because an administrative department is "costing the company too much." However, if the annual cost includes prorated expenses in the budget, the criticism is unrealistic and disingenuous: If the department is operating within its assigned costs, how can it cost "too much"? A portion includes an accounting journal entry rather than what the department actually spends, thus subverting the real purpose of budgeting. The criticism of the department manager would be fair if the department's budget included only items the manager was able to control, but placing the prorated expenses into the budget by way of an annual journal entry only causes problems and reduces the accuracy of financial review.

As long as the purpose of budgeting is to provide managers with the information they need to monitor internal controls and to hold down expenses, budgeting is a worthwhile pursuit. In many organizations, the so-called information supply chain is corrupted because budgets are based not on a manager's realistic capability to reduce expenses, but on a series of assigned budget items that cannot be controlled at all.

CALCULATING VARIANCES

The ultimate purpose of the budget is not to avoid variances that have to be explained. It is to identify problem areas as early as possible so that corrective action can be taken. The budget is a mechanism for expense control, not simply a compliance device to identify expense levels in advance and then adhere to them. So calculating budget variances is the key to monitoring expense levels and controlling them effectively. However, the budget is useless without the required follow-up action. A monthly report summarizing actual, budgeted, and variance figures has to be prepared, and then you need to determine what you need to do to fix problems.

To calculate a budget variance, first list the expenses as they have been reported for the month, and then list the month's budget items.

This step raises an important point: Do you study only the month's numbers, or do you base your budget analysis on year-to-date? The advantage of the monthly analysis is that it shows progress for that month. A disadvantage is that it ignores past variances and does not allow you to explain that some items are merely timing differences. An actual expense might not be booked in the month it is budgeted. For this reason, an adjusted year-to-date analysis of both actual and budgeted figures makes the most sense. To calculate year-to-date expenses, add the current month's total to the prior year-to-date total.

Year-to-Date Expense

$C + Y = E$

where: C = current month expense
Y = prior year-to-date expense
E = year-to-date expense

On a spreadsheet, list each expense item in its own column and enter:

A1   C
B1   Y
C1   = SUM(A1 + B1)

▶ Example: Your prior year-to-date expense for telephone was $2,815. This month's expense is $1,192. The year-to-date expense is:

$1,192 + $2,815 = $4,007

To calculate the year-to-date budget, add the current month to the prior year-to-date total.

Year-to-Date Budget

$C + Y = B$

where: C = current month budget
Y = prior year-to-date budget
B = year-to-date budget

On a spreadsheet, list each budget item in its own column and enter:

A1   C
B1   Y
C1   = SUM(A1 + B1)

▶ Example: This month's budget is $1,260. Your prior year-to-date budget for telephone was $2,550. The year-to-date budget is:

$1,260 + $2,550 = $3,810

The variance report consists of identifying significant variances and explaining them, whether favorable or unfavorable. You need to identify a significant variance as a starting point. You have no need to explain minor variations, which are going to occur in just about every expense category. The definition relies on the overall size of your expenses.

▶ Example: If your monthly expenses average $3,000, a variance of $100 might be considered significant. If your monthly expenses average $30,000, a $100 variance might not be worth analyzing.

A typical definition of a *significant variance* is any variance of $300 or more *and* 5% or more above or below the budget. This definition requires two tests. If the variance is above $300 but under the 5% threshold, it should not be analyzed under this definition.

To calculate a variance, compute the difference between actual expenses and budgeted expenses year-to-date.

Expense Variance

$$B - E = V$$

where: B = year-to-date budget
E = year-to-date expense
V = variance

On a spreadsheet, enter the following for each expense line item:

```
A1    B
B1    E
C1    = SUM(A1-B1)
```

If the value of V is positive, then it is a favorable variance; the budget total is higher than actual expenses. However, even a favorable variance should be studied and explained as long as it is significant. It could be caused by a timing problem between months or by faulty assumptions during budget preparation.

A negative value of V is an unfavorable variance and has to be explained, as long as it meets the definition of a significant variance.

▶ Example: You have defined a significant variance as any variance of 5% or more higher or lower than the year-to-date budget and of $100 or more. At the end of March, your year-to-date budget for telephone expense is $3,810, and actual telephone expenses year-to-date are $4,007. Your budget variance year-to-date is:

$3,810 − $4,007 = −$197

To calculate the percentage by which the variance is higher or lower than the budget, divide the year-to-date variance by the year-to-date budget.

Percentage of Expense Variance

$V \div B = P$

where: V = year-to-date variance (favorable or unfavorable)
B = year-to-date budget
P = percentage of expense variance

On a spreadsheet:

```
A1    V
B1    B
C1     = SUM(A1/B1)
```

▶ Example: The outcome is a significant variance because it meets both tests. It is higher than 5% of the year-to-date budget ($197 ÷ $3,810 = 5.2%), and the amount is greater than $100. It requires an explanation.

REVISING BUDGETS

The budget is not a process you execute once or twice per year and then forget about. Used effectively, the budget is a monitoring tool for controlling expenses and for spotting trends early enough to curtail excessive losses. Too often, budgets are imposed on managers with an expectation that somehow they will keep expenses within the mandated constraints, but without the control needed to accomplish that goal. This is a mistake. To work as intended, the budget has to be properly documented and used every month. And, upon discovery of an expense overrun, action has to be taken.

No matter how much groundwork goes into the budget, you are going to discover errors and changed circumstances. Anticipating the future for more than a few months due to ever changing competitive, market, and economic conditions is impossible. So, although an annual budget is prepared at the beginning of each year, a six-month revision is necessary. Remember that the purpose of the budget is to set a standard for keeping expenses under control. After six months, you will spot new trends and recognize flaws in the original budget. The reason for a revision is to reset the budget to a more accurate base, not to move expense levels up to accommodate out-of-control expense spending.

Budgeted expenses should be revised when:

1. *Conditions in your company have changed, making the original budget obsolete.* The market and competitive factors you face are constantly changing, and your company is changing as well. In a free enterprise environment, change is a constant, and, even in a controlled system, nothing remains the same for long. Even governmental management involves the continual adjustment of budgets as revenue moves upward or downward due to political and economic conditions. In other words, no company can operate for long in isolation. A 12-month budget is essential for setting annual goals, but after six months it is almost always outdated. Any expense whose original budget is no longer applicable to circumstances needs revision. For example, if revenues have risen far above expectations and internal staffing has been increased as a result, all expenses budgeted on a per-employee usage basis are now outdated.
2. *Mergers or disposals of operating segments have changed the landscape.* Your company may close a merger or acquisition deal with another firm, resulting in the consolidation of departments in a newly centralized location; or an operating segment may be sold off during the year. Both of these changes make the existing budget obsolete. Even if the change does not affect your immediate budget directly, newly structured profit and loss assumptions, increased or reduced goals, different levels of proration, and even changes in accounting methods all mean the current budget has to be revised and replaced.

3. *New internal controls or processes have been put in place.* You may experience a complete replacement of internal controls or processes. This occurs due to advice from independent auditors and systems consultants, regulatory or legal mandates, improved internal processing methods, adjustments in the supply chain, and even changes instituted by suppliers or vendors. Nothing is permanent and managers have to continually seek ways to hold down expenses. The budget is the monitoring device, but whenever change is imposed on the operational model, the budget has to be changed to reflect the new reality.

4. *Departments have been merged or otherwise changed.* In the interest of efficiency, management may change the definition of internal departments or segments. Simply combining two departments into one invariably results in a reduction of workforce, changes in processing, and an entirely different set of budget assumptions for most line items. For example, the consolidation of two marketing branches can reduce the need for separate processing by the administration of the company, the reduction or reassignment of the sales force, and fewer personnel for tracking, accounting, and servicing departments. Expanding the branch system may create the need for increased departmental payroll and other expenses, and even the segmenting of current support staff into new configurations.

Changes such as these make the current budget useless. Every change in the configuration of the company is going to have a direct effect on the budgets of most, if not all, departments. For this reason, six-month revisions—at the least—have to be assumed as necessary.

The revision should never be undertaken simply to adjust for discovered errors or to absorb unfavorable variances. Revision is effective only when used to find ways to fix expense overruns or to replace existing budgets with more realistic assumptions.

THE NATURE OF REVENUE FORECASTS

Forecasting revenue is quite different from budgeting expenses. In an expense budget, assumptions are defined by the nature of the expense and only a few bases are applicable. So, for example, assumptions using square feet are used to allocate or prorate utilities or printing. The number of employees often determines the budget for office supplies, telephone, and other varying expenses. Items like rent are often predetermined by contract. Another assumption base is proration, with some expenses assigned to departments on the basis of square footage or number of employees.

When it comes to forecasting revenue, however, an entirely different series of assumptions apply, based on the nature of the organization, the product or service marketed, and the kind of competitive environment. Here are some examples of appropriate assumptions:

1. *Salespersons' Activity and History.* In any company relying on a sales force or branch office system, notably those based on commission compensation, many marketing activities promote greater volume. The use of commission incentives or awards can produce exceptional volume in target periods.
2. *Market Share and Trend.* How does your organization compare to other companies marketing the same products or services? There is a real limit on how much market share a company will be able to capture. Is the market itself expanding or fixed? If sales are based on changes in population in a market region, then the changes should be taken into consideration when forecasting revenue growth. Is the existing trend positive? If so, will it continue and to what extent? In tracking a revenue trend, remember two key elements. First, market share is finite. Second, any trendline is going to level out in the future; no rate of growth can continue indefinitely.
3. *Product or Service Line Expansion.* Are the products or services you offer expanding or remaining at present levels? Without expansion, revenue growth is going to top out at some point. Even an expanded product or service line requires time to show up on the books. Remember that expanding the market may consist of gaining more customers or offering existing customers more in the future than in the past.
4. *Seasonal Variation.* In preparing your forecast, take seasonal variation into account. Most organizations, especially those marketing products, experience high- and low-volume periods. You cannot realistically expect to spread a forecast evenly throughout the year. It makes more sense to study past monthly volume and then apply the curve of the seasonal change to your new forecast. This

approach helps not only to place the right forecast level into the right season, but also to compare year-to-year outcomes to better track and anticipate revenue growth.

5. *Planned Acquisitions or Sales.* If your company is going to acquire or merge with another company during the year, the forecast may need to be put on a provisional basis. One outcome is expected to occur if the merger goes ahead, and another is expected if it does not. The same applies if you expect to sell off a segment during the coming year. If the sale does not take place, revenue should be forecast with existing assumptions. If the sale does occur, revenue (as well as costs and expenses) may be expected to decline immediately after the sale.

6. *Existing Trend.* The existing trend dictates all of the assumptions going forward. A revenue forecast cannot be based on the assumption that the existing trend is going to continue without slowdown; the trend has to be realistically leveled out. The forecast also has to be modified to account for the addition of new markets, products, or services, as well as for changes in competition (due to mergers or sales).

A revenue forecast also requires the tracking of direct costs. These are tied directly to revenue and therefore should be fairly easy to estimate. However, some factors are going to alter your direct cost estimates:

1. *Changes in the Long-Term Trend.* Have your direct costs remained constant for the past few years? Or have they been changing? For many internal and external reasons, the gross profit you book may be evolving over time. Do not assume that the trend will remain unchanged unless you have strong proof that it is a constant. In organizations providing services rather than products, direct costs are less of a factor than for those manufacturing, transporting, and selling tangible products.

2. *Known Changes in Merchandise Costs.* Will your suppliers continue to provide merchandise to you at the same cost level as in the past? Have cost increases been reflected in higher retail prices? Have your manufacturing or labor costs changed? You need to examine your cost assumptions. If you are booking a lower gross profit than in the

past, should you be marking up your prices to make up the
difference?

3. *Changes in the Product Mix.* If you are selling a more diverse range
of products today than in the past, the long-term trend could be
unreliable. If newly added products require a different level of costs
and if these new products represent a growing percentage of total
revenue, then historical cost ranges are not accurate.

4. *Adjustments in the Supply Chain and Inventory Practices.* With global
supply chains becoming more common than ever, you need to
consider within the cost of goods sold a broad range of costs and
possible changes. These include overseas manufacturing trends,
labor issues, warehousing, transportation, and related supply chain
risks that can affect your ability to meet demand and to keep costs
under control. In an income/cost forecast, including a contingent
cost for supply chain risks and possible losses only makes sense.

LOOKING AHEAD

Many forecasting and budgeting tasks require the study of trends, the
use of averages, and making allowances for change. All of these, like so
many of your tasks, require a basic understanding of statistics. The next
chapter explains the statistical formulas and applications every manager
needs to know.

C H A P T E R   1 0

Statistics for Effective Reporting

Beyond the realm of the familiar math involving financial reporting, marketing, and budgeting is the more complex world of *statistics*. A few important management applications require basic statistical skills. This chapter explains these skills and how they apply to you in your role as manager.

With statistics, your goal should be to find ways to simplify and clarify information while improving accuracy. Statistics too often have the opposite effect of alienating the recipient rather than providing an enlightened and improved summary of facts. The statistical processes you use should accomplish the goal of clarifying information instead of complicating it.

MANAGEMENT APPLICATION OF STATISTICS

Most managers are continually awash in numbers, projections, trends, and reports. You cannot avoid statistics, but you do need to master them. You do not need to get an advanced degree, but you should know a few important formulas. You are going to need statistics in budgeting, marketing, testing, risk management, and virtually any other facet of management involving judgments about dollar value, employees, trends, and profitability.

By definition, *statistics* consists of a set of information based on numbers. As a process, statistics is the method of analysis. As a set of numerical values, statistics can lead to conclusions based on the manipulation of those values. The process is necessary to test a sample of a larger base because it is not always practical to study all of your data. For example, a product test in 15 markets involving over 10,000 potential customers is going to generate a lot of information. Thus, with a properly designed survey, you can test a sample of the larger population. The proper use of a statistical sample requires that you identify methods to accurately test a small sample and ensure that it represents the overall population accurately.

▶ Example: A food company wants to test a new product before mass-producing it. So a test run is set up in several retail outlets. All the tests are performed at 5:30 P.M. on weekdays. Customers are asked to try a sample and answer three short questions:

    A. Do you like the taste?

    B. Would you buy this brand instead of the brand you now use?

    C. What is the most important to you: taste, price, or ingredients?

The results of the survey indicate that the product would do very well. However, when the product is placed on the market, results are dismal. The new product failed to compete with other brands and turned out to be an expensive mistake.

The mistake was in the formulation of the test itself. At 5:30 P.M. on weekdays, most of the shoppers were spouses on their way home from work who had been given a short list of necessities to buy. They were not their families' primary shoppers. The test sample consisted of shoppers who were attracted to taste, whereas the primary shoppers were more concerned with healthy ingredients and had a brand loyalty. On that basis, the new product did not perform well in the larger market.

This example demonstrates that picking an accurate sample from a large population is a very difficult task and demands great care.

A related problem is how questions are structured. The selection of words and phrasing often affects how a person will answer. This is a continual problem in political surveys.

▶ Example: Consider the following two versions of how the same question can be asked to affect the outcome:

- Version 1: Are you in favor of improved road systems in the county?
- Version 2: Do you think your taxes should be raised 30% to pay for new works projects?

Both versions may be part of a survey aimed at the same sample and concerning the same political issue. Version 1 is going to get a much higher rate of yes answers than version 2 because the emphasis is on road improvement. In version 2, the emphasis is placed on tax increases.

These issues point out some of the many problems in the use of statistics. A number of factors can alter the outcome of a data test. So whether you are working with market surveys or the result of financial data, finding an honest and consistent method for analyzing data is not as easy as many people think.

When using statistics, your management task involves three keys:

1. *How and where do you gather your data?* Some information is obvious, such as financial results or manufacturing productivity. If you need to know the size of a department or an average monthly expense, the information is easily obtained. Other information is more elusive, such as customer preferences or the forecasting of future production. If you want to know something in the future, you can use statistics to make estimates, but you are dealing with the unknown. The "facts" may be vastly different from what you think they are.

2. *How do you use or arrange facts?* The product marketing survey example makes the point that focusing on the wrong customer is going to affect the outcome. That test would have been more reliable if it had been performed at many different hours and days. Just because a sample produces a specific result does not mean the entire population will duplicate it. Accuracy relies on dedicated work in

identifying the right facts, as well as on how and when they are produced.

3. *What is the right question?* The food test example also focused on taste but did not ask the right question.

▶ Example: Perhaps a more reliable series of questions would have been:

    A. Are you the primary food buyer for your family?

    B. If so, what is the most important factor affecting what you buy? (Choices: taste, price, ingredients, packaging, product or brand loyalty)

    C. How does this product compare?

    D. Would you buy it instead of your current brand?

The accuracy of a sample is the most difficult aspect of a survey because, if you do not have an accurate sample, then the results are meaningless. Second, what you test and how questions are posed also affect the outcome. Coming up with a neutral question is very difficult, which is why questions are best if they are designed to be as neutral as possible in order to ensure that the sample is representative and will not affect outcome and that the whole effort does not create or cause bias in the results.

▶ Example: Asking grocery store shoppers if they are the primary buyers would eliminate those who are not, making the results more reliable. In the road improvement tax example, a first question might have been, "Do you plan to vote next Tuesday?"

Also affecting results is location. Is your political sample taken at a local university campus or in a retirement community? Obviously, these two populations are vastly different, pointing to the need to subdivide a sample by age group, income, and political affiliation. This requirement is not unique to political questions; the same distinctions are needed in all types of statistical sampling tests.

Statistical sampling is based on the rules of probability; the statistical inference is a testing of a sample to ensure that the sample is representative and that the outcome's probabilities are accurate. As long as the sample and test are well defined and accurately developed, you can esti-mate the probability of outcomes. The *law of large numbers* is used in many applications. The 50-50 choice is the best example of how this works. If you flip a coin a few times, you might get more heads or tails, but if you flip the coin thousands of times, the average outcome will become increasingly closer to the expected 50-50 result.

This rule applies to more complex calculations than the 50-50 chance of a coin toss. For example, when analyzing the risk of a loss, a manager needs to decide which risks to insure and which ones to transfer, miti-gate, or self-insure. The decision should be made on the likelihood of outcomes. So a plant accident needs to be insured because, over time, there is a high likelihood of occurrence. The threat of piracy or hijacking is relatively low, especially if the transport of finished goods is very lim-ited and local.

To ensure that you use statistics in the best possible way, while keeping it simple and manageable, you need to identify and impose a few smart ground rules:

1. *Be sure you understand the meaning of statistical terms.* Words like *sample* and *population* have very specific meanings. Statistics involves many other terms and requires careful distinctions among them.
2. *Test concepts and outcomes at every stage.* The field of statistics demands an exact discipline. Nothing can be assumed, and no outcome may be anticipated. It is never possible to remain completely neutral, but the scientific method required for honest statistical analysis also requires following the procedure without seeking a desired result.
3. *Question any outcome that seems wrong.* Your instincts are usually right, and if a statistical result is so far off that it raises questions, you probably need to review your information again and look for errors.

STATISTICAL AVERAGES

In previous chapters, the concepts of the simple and weighted average were introduced and explained. In statistics, the use of averages is common. However, it is more often called the *mean*, which is the same concept. In fact, you should be aware of three statistical ideas: mean, median, and mode. Each involves finding various types of midpoints in a field of values, and each is calculated in a different manner.

Median

The *median* is different from the mean (average). It represents the exact midpoint in a group of values (the *field*).

▶ Example: In a group of seven values, the median is the fourth value because there are three values above and three values below.

If the total values are even-numbered, the median is the average of the two values closest to the middle.

▶ Example: In a field of six values, the median is the average between values three and four.

You often hear this term used in economic reports. You hear about the average wage, but the median home price.

Median

$(F \div 2) + 0.5 = M$

where: F = field of values
         M = closest whole number to median

On a spreadsheet:

```
A1    F
B1    = SUM(A1/2) + .05
```

▶ Example: If the field includes an odd number of values, the median is rounded up. If there are seven values, the median is:

$(7 \div 2) + 0.5 = 4$

If the field includes an even number, the same formula works. You need to find the average of the two values closest to the middle. Thus, if there are eight values in the field, median is:

$(8 \div 2) + 0.5 = 4.5$

Mode

The *mode* is another variation by which statisticians report about a large field of values. Mode is the number that appears most often. It is not truly an average or a midpoint (like the median), but only the value that shows up most frequently. The value of mode is most apparent when an answer indicates outcomes like frequency.

▶ Example: A test contains the question, "How many telephone calls do you place each day from work?" The range of answers could be quite large, and both average and median will be less meaningful than the mode. So a "typical" telephone use is more accurately represented by means of mode for some types of questions. When you read a report that "the *average* employee makes four phone calls per day," that is entirely different from the result, "the *typical* employee makes three phone calls per day." In this example, the typical phone usage (mode) is a better indicator of future expectation than the average, which could be distorted by exceptionally high phone usage by a minority of people in the employee pool.

▶ Example: In the following field of values:

2, 3, 5, 5, 6, 8, 15

the mode is 5 because it appears twice, whereas all of the other values appear only once.

If a field contains more than one mode, the mode is the average of the two.

▶ Example: In the following field of values:

2, 3, 5, 5, 6, 6, 15

both 5 and 6 appear twice, tying for the mode. So the mode is 5.5.

Mean

The *mean* is identical to the average; however, many applications of statistics use a particular formula for weighting the average: the *expo-*

nential moving average (EMA). This is simply a method for adding more weight to the most recent values, but without having to go through a complex series of long calculations. Because the EMA can be calculated quickly, it is valuable for calculations involving a large number of fields, especially with new data constantly being added. In the basic moving average formula, you need to go through a series of calculations that become time-consuming.

▶ Example: You are figuring out the weighted average for a series of five fields. The manual calculation calls for adding twice the value of the most recent field. So each month, the oldest field is dropped and the newest one added. Over a period of months the values are:

Month	Values
January	1,604
February	1,715
March	1,892
April	1,854
May	1,899
June	1,846
July	1,900

Five fields are to be used each month. A weighted average providing greater weight for the latest entries in May, June, and July produces these results:

May: [1,604 + 1,715 +1,892 + 1,854 + (1,899 × 2)]
÷ 6 = 1,811
June: [1,715 + 1,892 + 1,854 + 1,899 + (1,846 × 2)]
÷ 6 = 1,842
July: [1,892 + 1,854 + 1,899 + 1,846 + (1,900 × 2)]
÷ 6 = 1,882

The totals are divided by six due to the weighting of the most recent value. This is how a weighted average is calculated without EMA. To make things easier, EMA is a form of shorthand for calculating a weighted moving average. The value 2 is first divided by the number of values in the field. Next, the average is calculated without any weighting. Then the first average is subtracted from the newest value, and that is multiplied by the result of the first step. The formula for the exponent is:

Exponent (Used in EMA)

$2 \div n = E$

where: n = total number of values in the field
E = exponent used in EMA calculation

Entries on a spreadsheet:

A1   N
A2   = SUM(2/A1)

The exponent for the calculation of weighted average over five periods is:

$2 \div 5 = 0.40$

The next step is to calculate the average of the five fields, as a starting point. The first set of five periods (January through May) produces a simple average of:

January–May: $(1{,}604 + 1{,}715 + 1{,}892 + 1{,}854 + 1{,}899) \div 5 = 1{,}793$

The next two months are June (1,846) and July (1,900). To convert the simple average into EMA, the average is the starting point. Next, the difference between the next field (in this case, 1,846) and the previous average is calculated:

$1{,}846 - 1{,}793 = 53$

This is multiplied by the exponent:

$53 \times 0.40 = 21$

This result is added to the previous average to arrive at the new exponential moving average:

$21 + 1{,}793 = 1{,}814$

The three-step process is repeated for the next month, where the value is 1,900:

1,900 − 1,814 = 86
86 × 0.40 = 34
34 + 1,814 = 1,848

This procedure is repeated indefinitely for as many additions as are needed for the exponential moving average over many subsequent periods. The first step—calculating the simple average—has to be performed only once, at the beginning. And the last step, the entry of the new field, also has to be performed only once. The formula appears more complex than it is because the calculation of average is included twice.

Exponential Moving Average (EMA)

$$(\{V_p - [(V_1 + V_2 + \ldots V_n \div n]\} \times (2 \div n)) + P = E$$

where: V_p = previous EMA
$\quad V_1$ = first value in the field
$\quad V_2$ = second value in the field
$\quad V_n$ = last value in the field
$\quad n$ = number of values in the field
$\quad P$ = previous EMA
$\quad E$ = new EMA

The entries on the spreadsheet are:

A1 THROUGH A_N	VALUES IN THE FIELD ('N' IS THE TOTAL NUMBER OF FIELDS)
B1	= SUM(($A1:A_N$)/N)
C1	= SUM(2/N)
D1	= V_2 (NEXT VALUE IN THE FIELD)
E1	= SUM(D1-B1)
F1	= (SUM(E1*C1)
G1	= SUM(F1 + B1)

The formula first develops the average for the initial field and then develops it for subsequent fields with a single new cell entry.

▶ Example: Using the spreadsheet cells with the previous example's information, the cell contents are:

	A	B	C	D	E	F
1	1,604	1,793	0.40	1,846	53	1,814
2	1,715	1,814	0.40	1,900	86	1,848
3	1,892					
4	1,854					
5	1,899					

The contents of all of the A cells and of the two D cells are entered; the rest are the result of applying the cell formulas. The contents of F cells are the EMA results.

Calculations of median, mode, and EMA are used for subsequent statistical computations, especially in the study of how values change or are dispersed through a range of possible outcomes. For example, in a marketing study of customer preferences, you expect to receive a range of responses from one extreme to another. In this process, you need to identify the most common response to determine the "typical" preferences.

DISPERSION, VARIANCE, AND DEVIATION

Dispersion

In statistics, the analysis of dispersion is a key concept. *Dispersion* (also called *spread*) is the degree of difference between the values in a field and the average of the field. It is a very important concept because it identifies how future changes can be predicted. The greater the dispersion you find, the greater the possibility of future variance away from the average. So the measurement of dispersion is a scientific way to measure predictability.

One of the best ways to reduce the reported volatility in a field of values is to apply a basic statistical standard: removal of the extremes. By taking out the exceptionally high value and the exceptionally low value, you narrow down the range and make the dispersion easier to identify.

▶ Example: You are estimating the number of employees you expect to have in your division for the coming year. Over the past six months, the number ranged between 6 and 37:

Month	Employees
July	6
August	35
September	26
October	27
November	37
December	35

Of these six months, the first (July) is not typical. This may have resulted from a start-up when only a few employees were on hand, thus making it atypical of what you expect for the future. As a result, you exclude July's number from your total and calculate only the average of the remaining five months.

Using only the five typical-range values reduces future unpredictability, especially in calculating what is called the *mean absolute deviation*. This measures the degree of distance from each value from the overall mean (average). The first step is to measure the difference itself; the next is to square that difference. The values are:

Month	Employees	Mean	Difference	Square
August	35	32	3	9
September	26	32	6	36
October	27	32	5	25
November	37	32	5	25
December	35	32	3	9
Total				104

The difference is the key element; it does not matter whether it is positive or negative. The next step is to find the mean (average) of the squared values:

$$(9 + 36 + 25 + 25 + 25) \div 5 = 24$$

The result of the averaging, 24, is called the *dispersion factor*. By itself, the value is meaningless. But it is the first step in the calculation of the variance from the mean, and that is used to predict the volatility of future forecasts.

Mean Absolute Deviation

$$[(V_1 - A)^2 + (V_2 - A)^2 + \ldots (V_n - A)^2] \div n = D$$

where: V_1 = first value in the field
        A = average of the field
        V_2 = second value in the field
        V_n = last value in the field of n
        n = number of values in the field
        D = mean absolute deviation

On a spreadsheet, the values are:

A1 THROUGH A$_N$ V (ONE VALUE PER CELL THROUGH CELL N)
B1   A
                   COPY B1 AND PASTE FOR ALL B CELLS
C1 THROUGH C$_N$ = SUM(A1-B1)*(A1-B1)
                   COPY C1 AND PASTE FOR ALL C CELLS
D1   = SUM(C1:C8)/8

Example: Using the same information, the resulting cell contents are:

	A	B	C	D
1	35	32	9	21
2	26	32	36	
3	27	32	25	
4	37	32	25	
5	35	32	9	

Variance

An alternative method for arriving at the same result is the calculation of variance. In this process, you find the square of each value in the field and then divide the results to find the average. Then the square of the original average is subtracted.

▶ Example: In the previous example, the average was 32; so the square was 1,024 (32 × 32).

The formula for variance is:

Variance

$$\{[(V_1)^2 + (V_2)^2 + \ldots (V_n)^2] \div n\} - (V_1 + V_2 + \ldots V_n)^2 = VR$$

where: V_1 = first value in the field
V_2 = second value in the field
V_n = last value in the field of n values
N = number of values in the field
VR = variance

On a spreadsheet:

A1 THROUGH A$_N$ VALUES
B1   +SUM(A1:A$_N$)/N
C1   SUM(A1-B1)*(A1-B1)
   COPY C1 AND PASTE TO REMAINING C CELLS
D1   SUM(C1:C$_N$)/N

Variance is a relatively easy and fast calculation, but it ends up with the same answer as the calculation of mean absolute deviation. By whichever route you arrive at this answer, it is an important quantity because it is used to calculate *standard deviation*, which is the ultimate degree of uncertainty about the future values. When used in budgeting and forecasting, this is a method for identifying the degree of certainty in the estimates you use.

BASIC MATH REVIEW

The square root is the inverse value of the square, or any number multiplied by itself and expressed as n^2. The square root is used in many statistical and geometric calculations and, when it is used, the symbol v is the proper indicator. This symbol asks the question, "What number, multiplied by itself, equals the principal value?" For example, $v25 = 5$ because $5 \times 5 = 25$.

Deviation

Statisticians use the Greek lowercase symbol *sigma* (σ) to represent standard deviation. The calculation requires you to first figure the square root of the variance, and then divide by the average of the field.

Standard Deviation

$$\sqrt{v}$$

On a spreadsheet:

A1   SQRT(v)

▶ Example: In the previous example, the variance was 21. So the deviation is the square root of that value:

$$\sqrt{21} = 4.6$$

Replying on the established formulas in many spreadsheet programs, this is fairly easy to calculate. Excel, for example, uses the preset formula $= \mathrm{SQRT}(v)$. Enter 21 within the parentheses:

A1 $= \mathrm{SQRT}(21)$

The standard deviation is next divided by the average of the previous field, to arrive at the percentage known as the dispersion factor.

Dispersion Factor

$$\sqrt{v} \div [(V_1 + V_2 + \ldots V_n)] \div n = D$$

where: $\sqrt{v}$ = variance
V_1 = first value in a field of values
V_2 = second value in a field of values
n = number of values in the field
D = dispersion factor

On a spreadsheet:

A1	$= \text{SQRT}(v)$
B1 THROUGH B$_N$	VALUES
C1	$= \text{SUM}(B1:B_N)/N$
D1	$= \text{SUM}(A1/C1)$

Example: Using the information from the previous example, the formula is:

$$\sqrt{21} \div [(35 + 26 + 27 + 37 + 35) \div 5] = 14.4\%$$

With this percentage, developed from manipulating the values in the field, you can draw meaningful conclusions:

1. The range used was between 26 and 37, excluding an exceptionally low month as nontypical.
2. The dispersion of this range is a value of 11, or the net difference between the highest and lowest numbers.
3. The variance factor is 21, as calculated by either mean absolute deviation or variance.
4. The calculation produces a dispersion of 4.6 employees (the square root of 21).
5. The dispersion in the list is equal to 14.4%.

The significance of these values depends on the size of the numbers and on the reliability of estimates within the budget or forecast. In calculating the number of employees you expect to hire in the next year, the relative volatility is 14.4% based on recent historical data. In comparing volatility between different account classifications or even among departments, you may find higher or lower volatility, indicating the degree of overall reliability. For areas with higher volatility, the indication may be that you need to perform a more detailed analysis to bring down the level of volatility.

The example is a fairly limited one. However, when applied to larger fields of values or to less predictable areas of forecasting, the development of the dispersion factor is very valuable, especially in comparative form. This is why an important part of a statistical process is to test for errors in estimates.

ACCURACY IN STATISTICS

An estimate of the future outcome of anything (forecasts, budgets, cash flow, product sales) is going to contain a degree of deviation due to errors in assumptions and estimates. Statistics provides methods for explaining errors as reasonable or within a range of expectations. Measuring the range of deviations quantifies the error so that it can be compared to errors in other processes or to an accepted standard.

Beyond the few statistical formulas presented in this chapter, many more advanced processes are used to delve into expected levels of error versus actual outcomes. Unfortunately, the more complex the calculation is, the less likely it is that management will understand it. Most people do not appreciate statistical summaries because they are known to be based on probability analysis and sample testing. In other words, they cannot be used reliably to pinpoint an outcome. Even though no other process does better in narrowing down variation in outcome, statistical analysis is not widely appreciated.

The budgeting process is an excellent example of a struggle that managers are engaged in continually. No one can reliably identify the coming year's exact revenue, expenses, or profits. Too many variables are in play. Even the budgeting process itself affects outcomes. For example, if you forecast revenue based on an especially aggressive set of assumptions, word of the assumptions may filter out to the marketing force in the field and affect their behavior. Some aspects of forecasting and budgeting thus contain a degree of self-fulfilling prophecy, further complicating how assumptions are developed and applied. The same limitations apply to product testing, customer surveys, cash flow controls, production levels, and any other financial or numerical analysis.

Estimates cannot be avoided; they provide management with a means of setting goals and then monitoring progress. Whether the test is for revenue or profits, controls over cash flow, or success in a new product's market, estimates rely on detailed and logical assumptions, follow-up analysis and action, and an appropriate use of statistics. Even if you limit your analysis to relatively simple statistical tools like exponential moving averages or the calculation of dispersion factors, you still rely on accuracy in the underlying assumptions. Estimating and the related use of statistics provide many benefits to you as a manager.

1. Risk Analysis and Identification

Understanding the range of risks you face and how to deal with them is a pervasive and challenging management problem. With the advancement of global supply chains and reliance on international vendors, manufacturing, storage, and transportation, the risk universe has expanded in recent decades. You need to decide which risks to mitigate, insure, transfer, or accept without action. The decision relies on the likelihood of loss, the potential cost of an event, and your ability to affect the environment. These are big questions, and you cannot decide how to address risks (including possible unknown or unidentified risks) without detailed study.

The decision requires many forms of estimation, including statistical analysis. Insurance companies use statistical analysis to determine how much of a premium to charge and how much of a deductible and copay to require for a covered risk, as well as which risks to not even cover. The same approach has to be used for risks you decide to mitigate, transfer, or accept.

- You *mitigate* a risk by changing the environment to reduce exposure.
- You *transfer* a risk by passing it on to another entity (a subcontractor, vendor, or even your customer).
- You *accept* a risk by determining that a loss is unlikely and that the other choices are cost-prohibitive.

Advanced statistical analysis is likely to play an important role in this analysis, and you probably will rely on consultation with a risk management company or consultant. Nevertheless, it is instructive and necessary to understand how statistical analysis is performed to reach a conclusion. Just as your presentations or requests to management require explanation, when you work with someone else, you also need to understand how they develop their conclusions. Risk analysis is probably one of the most important undertakings for managers.

2. Quantifying the Feasibility of a Proposal

Managers are idea people. They are likely to put up proposals for changes in processes, cost cutting, internal controls, customer service, and improvements to the supply chain. All such proposals vary in their feasibility. They involve practical restrictions, costs, and time elements that determine whether the proposals make sense. So if you approach management with a proposal (or someone reporting to you comes forward with a proposal), these important considerations are present whether expressed or not.

A common response to an idea is, "What is this going to cost?" This is a central question, of course, and the answer is most likely to determine whether an idea is approved or rejected. However, additional questions should be addressed as well: "What restrictions or limits apply?" "How long will it take to implement?" If you keep these questions in mind, you will be more likely to quantify the feasibility of a proposal.

▶ Example: If a proposal is brought forward to combine two departments into one and reassign some employees, the issues worth studying are:

Cost:

- How much money will be saved by combining two departments?
- Are the savings permanent or will current expense levels return?
- What is the savings from reducing employee levels or higher efficiency of floor space?

Restrictions:

- Is it practical to combine these departments?
- What internal checks and balances might be compromised as a result?
- By how much will the idea eliminate duplication? Would alternative solutions cost less?

Time requirements:

- How long will it take to put this plan into effect?
- Will labor redundancies be absorbed through attrition and, if so, over what time period?
- What time span is involved in retraining employees?

3. Support for Proposals or Initiatives

In addition to deciding whether an idea is feasible, statistical analysis may help to make your case. When reviewing someone else's proposal, the same analysis may also be used to question whether the assumptions are rational and profitable.

▶ Example: In the case of combining departments, statistical study can be used to analyze current labor costs, estimate duplication of effort, and identify potential savings based on average wages. Additional savings may also come from higher efficiency in the use of floor space (such as deferring the need for more rental expense due to expansion in the future).

If a proposal is justified by limited savings, the potential savings versus likely inefficiency should be critically analyzed.

▶ Example: If a limited amount of monthly savings is compared to the one-time cost of making the change, how many months will it take to break even? By that time, will expansion require breaking apart the combined department due to increased workload?

A critical analysis of questions like this could make the decision less appealing due to only marginal potential benefits.

4. Establishing Standards

Statistical analysis has perhaps its greatest value when used to set standards. In a marketing forecast, you can support goals for a sales force based on volume of orders. In an expense budget, statistical reporting may be used to identify a reasonable level of expenses, providing you with the means for measuring variances throughout the year. In a production plant, the analysis of shift defects and productivity can identify the most likely problem areas or weak links and point to methods to reduce problems.

Statistics are used in just about every aspect of analysis involving the *p* numbers (production, personnel, and profits). Analysis is not simply a process undertaken by accountants and statisticians; it can also be applied to effectively reduce inefficiencies, avoid losses, bolster profitability, and make proposals convincing. All of these outcomes are the result of setting standards and demonstrating how they can be enforced for a better future outcome.

LOOKING AHEAD

One of the advantages of mastering math is that it improves your critical judgment and makes you comfortable with financial information, even when your background does not include financial analysis. You vastly improve your ability to use math when you know a few easy but valuable shortcuts. Among the most useful of shortcuts is the estimate of an answer to a problem. If your answer is close to the estimate, it is probably right. If it is off by millions, the chances are good that the calculation includes a serious error. It fails the so-called test of reasonableness. The next chapter concludes with some useful math shortcuts in the basic functions as well as conversions among percentages, decimals, and fractions.

Incredible Math Shortcuts

As a manager, you do not have to use a calculator or spreadsheet programming to figure out everything. Many shortcuts allow you to quickly and easily conquer the challenge of math.

This chapter lists many fast shortcuts in the first two basic functions: addition and subtraction. The purpose is to provide an overview of some of the more practical applications of math shortcuts, and there is more advantage to learning these than simply mastering some shortcuts. Math shortcuts also help you to:

- Estimate outcomes to avoid errors.
- Convert difficult numerical formats to more manageable ones before calculating answers.
- Master specific mathematical functions that have otherwise presented difficulties.

ADDITION SHORTCUTS

The first basic mathematical function is addition. In school you were taught to add using a well-known model, but it does not always guarantee fast results and is not necessarily the most efficient way to add.

Addition Shortcut 1: Adding from the Left

The traditional method involves first adding the far right column (the 1's), carrying over any digits beyond 9 and then repeating the process in the 10's column. The first shortcut is to abandon this system and add beginning on the *left* instead of on the right.

▶ Example: A typical math exercise calls for addition of three large numbers:

    8,416
    7,715
 + 4,499

The traditional method of carrying digits over looks like this:

  1 12
  8,416
  7,715
+ 4,499
20,630

Under the usual method, the process begins at the far right where the three digits are added: 6 + 5 + 9 = 20. The 0 is placed beneath the far right column and the 2 carried over as a remainder. Next, the 10s column is added, including the remainder: 1 + 1 + 9 + 2 = 13. The 3 is listed in the answer and the 1 is carried over to the 100's column. It is then added as well: 4 + 7 + 4 + 1 = 16. This process is repeated until you arrive at the answer of 20,630.

The problem with this traditional approach is that carrying remainders is where most people run into trouble. Unless you grasp the value of the "ones" and "tens" columns, carrying over remainders makes no sense; so as a result, students learn to follow steps because that's how it is done, without really understanding *why* it is necessary.

A solution is to get around the carrying of remainders entirely. By just adding up the value of each column, you can figure out the answer at least as quickly, and often more quickly, without having to perform any extra steps (like carrying of remainders).

Now try the problem by starting at the left and carrying a series of additions for each column, starting at the left:

	8416
	7715
	+ 4499
Add the far left column, $8+7+4$.	19
Add the second column from the left, $4+7+4$.	15
Then the third column, $1+1+9$.	11
Then the last column on the right, $6+5+9$.	20
Now add each column again.	1
Add 9 + 1.	10
5 + 1	6
1 + 2 and last column, 0	30
Now add up the results.	20630

The method takes up more space but does not involve more calculations, and no excess numerals need to be carried over as remainders. The steps go very quickly and result in improved accuracy as well.

Addition Shortcut 2: Rounding Up

Another shortcut requires that you round up numbers to be added and then subtract the amount rounded.

▶ Example: Here is a typical two-number addition problem:

37 + 49 = ?

This can be calculated easily enough but there is a quick shortcut as well. It requires you to round both numbers up to the next number divisible by 10:

▶ Example: 40 + 50 = 90

The answer is quite easy. The final step is to subtract the value of the rounded-up numbers. The first number, 37, was rounded up by 3, and the second, 49, was rounded up by 1. Subtract the total of 4 from the answer:

40 + 50 = 90 − (3 + 1) = 86

Both steps—rounding up and subtracting the rounded value—can be done in your head and require less thinking than the traditional method. This also works for three or more numbers. For example:

47 + 58 + 66 = ?

converts to

50 + 60 + 70 = 180 − (3 + 2 + 4) = 171

Addition Shortcut 3: Fast Addition in Steps

In this shortcut, you calculate the additional values of a series of numbers, one at a time, adding by 10s as well as by remainders.

▶ Example: When asked to add 37 and 49, you can quickly estimate the answer with a process of steps. This involves adding the components of 49 in 10s: 10, 20, 30, 40, and 49, but starting with 37 as the base:

37 + 10 = 47 + 10 = 57 + 10 = 67 + 10 = 77 + 9 = 86

It is a simple matter of mental adding. First, in your head, quickly compute:

37, 47, 57, 67, 77, 86

This seems like a lot of work just to add up two numbers, but it is the process you probably follow automatically without thinking about it. However, most people limit this technique to only two numbers. Now think about how you can apply the same shortcut to a larger series of two-digit numbers.

▶ Example:

47 + 58 + 66 = ?

Add the components of 58 to 47:

47: 57 (+10), 67 (+10), 77 (+10), 87 (+10), 97 (+10), 105 (+8)

Add the components of 66 to 105:

105: 115 (+10), 125 (+10), 135 (+10), 145 (+10), 155 (+10), 165 (+10), 171 (+ 6)

The process of adding in your head by 10s and then attaching the remaining value works for any size list of two-digit numbers.

Addition Shortcut 4: Fast Addition by Columns

The next shortcut breaks down the columns and adds them separately.

▶ Example:

47 + 58 + 66 = ?

First add the 10's columns and then add the 1's in sequence:

$$40 + 50 + 60 = 150 + 7 + 8 + 6 = 171$$

Number of steps: 90   150   157 165 171

This series of quick additions is easily done in your head and is a great exercise for improving rapid addition skills. Just looking at the columns of numbers, your fast mental addition takes you right to the total: 40, 90, 150, 157, 165, 171.

SUBTRACTION SHORTCUTS

With subtraction, students are taught to use a precise and consistent formula. Like addition, subtraction can be made easier with a few easy shortcuts.

Subtraction Shortcut 1: Add the Distances from 100

When you have to subtract two numbers, and one is above and the other is below 100 (or any other multiple of 100), you can use a fast shortcut to make subtraction easier.

▶ Example: You need to subtract 96 from 153 (this would also work with 196 and 253 because the distance between the two values is the same):

$$153 - 96 \ = 57$$
$$253 - 196 = 57$$

To calculate the answer, take the distance of each number from 100 and then add the two results:

$$153 - 100 = 53$$
$$100 - 96 \ = \ 4$$
$$53 \ + 4 \ \ = 57$$

This series of steps can often be performed in your head and more rapidly than the traditional method, which involves moving values between columns. The traditional method requires moving the value of 10 from the 10's column and adding it to the 1's column. This changes 3 to 13 to make it larger than the 1's column.

$$
\begin{array}{r}
153 \\
- 96 \\
\hline
\end{array}
\quad = \quad
\begin{array}{r}
14^{1}3 \\
- 9\ 6 \\
\hline
5\ 7
\end{array}
$$

This is a cumbersome series of steps that is difficult to teach and even more difficult to learn. It is much easier to rapidly isolate 53 and 4, and then add them.

Subtraction Shortcut 2: Alter Both Sides to Simplify

A second great shortcut, which also eliminates the carrying-the-10's problem, is to simply increase both numbers in order to round the number to be subtracted. Remember, when you change two numbers equally, the answer remains the same.

▶ Example: The subtraction 36 − 29 is identical to the value of 37 − 30. We have added 1 to both values, but the second version is easier to calculate:

$$36 - 29 = 7$$
$$37 - 30 = 7$$

The technique works in reverse as well.

▶ Example: Subtract 52 from 71 but *reduce* the values to the closest lower round number:

71 − 52 = 19
69 − 50 = 19

▶ The adjustment of the value to be subtracted, either up or down to a round number, greatly simplifies the process, making it much easier to quickly do the calculation in your head.

Subtraction Shortcut 3: Convert to Two Steps

When you have to move values from one column to another, you make a problem more complicated than it needs to be, especially when the subtraction task is presented in horizontal form. If you were taught to perform functions horizontally, the side-to-side format does not visually present you with a solution.

To overcome this difficulty, break down the subtraction problem into two easy steps. This works for any two two-digit values.

▶ Example: You have to subtract 37 from 82:

82 − 37 = 45

To easily perform this in your head, first subtract the 10's column from the lower value; then subtract the remainder:

Subtract the 10's column: 82 − 30 = 52
Subtract the 1's column: 52 − 7 = 45

Like the other methods, this one can be rapidly performed in your head, and you don't have to cancel out the value of 10 and transfer it to the 1's column. The preceding steps make it easy to perform the process in your head, even for three-digit values.

▶ Example:

191 − 126 = ?

Subtract the 10's column: 191 − 120 = 71
Subtract the 1's column: 71 − 6 = 65

This also works when the two values are not within the same 100s range:

▶ Example:

215 − 162 = ?

| Subtract the 10's column: | 215 − 160 = 55 |
| Subtract the 1's column: | 55 − 2 = 53 |

This is somewhat more difficult to perform mentally because of the gap between the two values. Even so, removing the need to carry over values greatly simplifies the entire subtraction process.

Shortcuts come in handy for adding and subtracting, but they can be essential when dealing with the more complex formulas for multiplication and division. Multiplication has to begin with an explanation of a few logical rules.

LOGICAL RULES

When you move beyond adding and subtracting and start multiplying numbers, you face more potential problems. Most people have some level of difficulty with multiplication, but using some simple shortcuts vastly simplifies the process.

First, a few logical multiplication rules need to be reviewed to take a lot of mystery out of multiplication.

Equivalents in Multiplication

if	A	=	B
and	A	=	C
then	B	=	C

where: A, B, and C = any values

To check the validity of these logical statements on a spreadsheet:

A1	A
B1	B
C1	C
A2	= SUM(A1*B1)
B2	= SUM(A1*C1)
C2	= SUM(B1*C1)

In other words, the equality of two related values dictates the third value as well. Another involves multiplication by the values of 0 and 1:

Multiplication by 0 and 1:

$A \times 0 = 0$
$A \times 1 = A$

where: A = any value

Check this on a spreadsheet:

A1   A
B1 $= SUM(A1*0)$
B2 $= SUM(A1*1)$

Summarizing these two universal truths, any value multiplied by 0 is always equal to 0. And any number multiplied by 1 is always equal to the number itself (A).

In a similar manner, another series of logical statements relate to multiplying by positive or negative values:

Multiplication of Positive and Negative Values

$P_1 \times P_2 = P$
$P \times N = N$
$N_1 \times N_2 = P$

where: P = positive value
        N = negative value

On a spreadsheet:

A1 P_1 (FIRST POSITIVE VALUE)
A2 P_2 (SECOND POSITIVE VALUE
A3 N_1 (FIRST NEGATIVE VALUE)
A4 N_2 (SECOND NEGATIVE VALUE)
B1 $= SUM(A1*A2)$
C1 $= SUM(A1*A3)$
D1 $= SUM(A3*A4)$

A positive value multiplied by another positive *always* results in a positive answer. When a positive is multiplied by a negative, it is always a negative answer. Finally, when a negative value is multiplied by another negative value, it is always a positive answer.

Finally, rules apply when multiplying even and odd numbers:

Multiplication by Even and Odd Values

$E_1 \times E_2 = E$

$E \times O = O$

$O_1 \times O_2 = O$

where: E = any even value

O = any odd value

On a spreadsheet:

A1 E_1 (FIRST EVEN VALUE)

A2 E_2 (SECOND EVEN VALUE)

A3 O_1 (FIRST ODD VALUE)

A4 O_2 (SECOND ODD VALUE)

B1 $=$ SUM(A1*A2)

C1 $=$ SUM(A1*A3)

D1 $=$ SUM(A3*A4)

In other words, all even numbers multiplied by any other even numbers always produce an even-numbered answer. However, in any operation involving any odd number, the answer will always be odd. This is true even if more than two values are in play.

Beyond the basic rules of multiplication are several useful shortcuts. These help clarify the process and enable you to perform many operations in your head.

MULTIPLICATION SHORTCUTS

Multiplying is a more complex process than adding or subtracting. The added complexity causes some people to have greater trouble with multiplication than they should. For example, they find it easier to add 23, 23, and 23; but multiplying 23 by 3 poses a greater problem. This learned inhibition can be undone with the help of some useful multiplication shortcuts.

Multiplication Shortcut 1: Squaring Numbers

One form of multiplication is squaring, or multiplying a number by itself:

Squaring a Number

$n^2 = S$

where: n = any value

   S = square of the value

On a spreadsheet program:

A1 $= \text{SUM}(\text{N}*\text{N})$

When you square any number ending in 5, there is a convenient shortcut. First, multiply the 10s digits by the next whole number. Then affix 25 to the result.

Square of Any Number Ending in 5

$t \times (n + 1){:}25 = n^2$

where: t = 10s value of the number to be squared

   n = number to be squared

   : = affix

To prove this on a spreadsheet:

A1 $= \text{SUM}(\text{N}*\text{N})$

▶ **Example: Calculate the square of 25:**

$25^2 = ?$

$2 \times 3 = 6$

6 affixed to 25 = 6:25, or 625

This works with any values.

▶ Example: Compute the square of 85.

$85^2 = ?$
$8 \times 9 = 72$
72 affixed to 25 = 72:25, or 7,225

▶ Another method involves squaring numbers ending in 1. In these cases, first drop the 1 from the value. Next, find the square of the rounded number. Then add the original number to the newly calculated number.

Square of Any Number Ending in 1

$(n - 1)^2 + [n + (n - 1)] = n^2$

where: n = number to be squared

To prove this on a spreadsheet:

A1 $= SUM(N*N)$

▶ Example: Find the square of 71:

$71^2 = ?$
$71 - 1 = 70$
$70^2 = 4,900$
$70 + 71 = 141$
$4,900 + 141 = 5,041$

The value 71 is converted to 70. When these two values are added to the square of 70, the answer is correct for 71^2. The technique is amazing and easy, but it always works.

Another nice squaring shortcut works when you need to find the answer for a number ending in 9. In this case, you increase the number to be squared by 1, to a round number. Then find its square, and add the original and the revised numbers. Finally, subtract the total from the square calculated in the first step.

Square of Any Number Ending in 9

$(n + 1)^2 - [n + (n + 1)] = n^2$

where: n = number to be squared

To prove this on a spreadsheet:

A1 $= \text{SUM}(N*N)$

▶ Example: Find the square of 79:

$79^2 = ?$
$79 + 1 = 80$
$80^2 = 6,400$
$80 + 79 = 159$
$6,400 - 159 = 6,241$

Another squaring technique works for any two-digit number starting with the digit 5. To perform this shortcut, first add 25 to the 1's digit. Then square the 1's digit (to two places) and affix that square to the answer in the first step.

▶ Example: Find the squares of 53, 55, and 57:

$53^2 = ?$
$3 + 25 = 28$
$3^2 = 09$
$28:09 = 2,809$

$55^2 = ?$
$5 + 25 = 30$
$5^2 = 25$
$30:25 = 3,025$

$57^2 = ?$
$7 + 25 = 32$
$7^2 = 49$
$32:49 = 3,249$

Multiplication Shortcut 2: Dropping the Zeroes

Whenever you have to multiply two numbers together and one or both contain an ending value of 0, the steps are simplified by dropping the 0's. The most basic version of this is multiplying two values.

▶ Example:

60 × 7 = ?

Drop the 0 and then add it back to the answer:

6 × 7 = 42
42 converts to 420

With only one 0 involved, this is a fairly easy process. However, when both values contain zeroes, you need to add them both.

▶ Example:

60 × 70 = ?

Drop the 0's and then add both of them back to the answer:

6 × 7 = 42
42 converts to 4,200

To make this easier to remember, add one 0 to the answer for each 0 dropped. This works for any extension.

▶ Example:

600 × 70 = ?

Drop all of the 0's and then add all of them back to the answer:

6 × 7 = 42
42 converts to 42,000

Multiplication Shortcut 3: Multiplying by 4

If you can multiply by 2, you can also multiply by 4. This involves two steps: First, double the number. Second, double again.

▶ Example:

62 × 4 = ?

The solution to perform in your head takes two steps, both doubling:

62 × 2 = 124
124 × 2 = 248

This process can be applied to any value multiplied by 4. However, as you get into larger numbers, it becomes more of a challenge.

Multiplication Shortcut 4: Multiplying by 5

The trick to multiplying by 5 is to remember that 5 is one-half of 10 and that multiplying by 10 is easy. You simply add a 0. This problem is solved in two ways; you can either multiply by 10 and then divide by 2, or you can first divide by 2 and then multiply by 10.

Multiplication by 5

$(n \times 10) \div 2 = a$

where: n = number ending in 5
a = answer

To prove on a spreadsheet:

A1 = SUM((N*10)/2)

Method 1:

22 × 5 = ?
22 × 10 = 220
220 ÷ 2 = 110

Method 2:

22 × 5 = ?
22 ÷ 2 = 11
11 × 10 = 110

The problem is more complex when multiplying an odd number. Dividing it by two as a first step results in a fraction or decimal value.

▶ Example: If you are multiplying 23 by 5, one-half of 23 is expressed as either 11½ or 11.5. For this reason, the easiest solution is to first multiply by 10. Any multiplication by an even number *always* produces an even number, making it easier to divide by 2:

$23 \times 5 = ?$
$23 \times 10 = 230$
$230 \div 2 = 115$

Multiplication Shortcut 5: Multiplying by 11

One shortcut appears magical because it is so easy and so fast. When multiplying any two-digit by 11, insert the sum of the multiplier's digits between them and you have the answer.

▶ Example: Multiply 27 by 11.

$2 + 7 = 9$

Convert 27 to 297.

This works for any multiplier whose digits add up to 9 or less. When the digits add up to 10 or more, the 1's digit of the answer is applied as in the preceding example, and the extra digit is carried to the left.

▶ Example: If you multiply 67 by 11.

$6 + 7 = 13$
Convert 67 to 6 3 7
Carry the 1:7 3 7

A second method is to multiply the number by 10 and then add the original number to the total.

▶ Example: Multiply 27 by 11.

$27 \times 10 = 270$
$270 + 27 = 297$

▶ Example: Multiply 67 by 11.

67 × 10 = 670
670 + 67 = 737

Multiplication Shortcut 6: Multiplying by 12

To multiply by 12, use the same procedure, but add the original number twice to the multiple by 10:

27 × 10 = 270
270 + 27 + 27 = 324

67 × 10 = 670
670 + 67 + 67 = 804

Multiplication Shortcut 7: Multiplying by 9

This trick is similar to multiplying by 11. The solution is to multiply the number by 10, and then subtract the original number from the total.

▶ Example: Multiply 27 by 9.

27 × 10 = 270
270 − 27 = 243

▶ Example: Multiply 67 by 9.

67 × 10 = 670
670 − 67 = 603

Multiplication Shortcut 8: Multiplying by 15

Multiplying by 15 is easy because it involves first multiplying by 10, or simply adding a 0, and then adding half of that total.

▶ Example: Multiply 27 by 15.

27 × 10 = 270
270 ÷ 2 = 135
270 + 135 = 405

▶ Example: Multiply 67 by 15.

    $67 \times 10 = 670$
    $670 \div 2 = 335$
    $670 + 335 = 1,005$

Multiplication Shortcut 9: Multiplying Two Numbers Two Digits Apart

Another impressive trick involves multiplying two numbers separated by two. Square the number between the two digits and then subtract 1 from the answer.

▶ Example: Multiply 25 by 27.

    $25 \times 27 = ?$
    $26^2 = 676$
    $676 - 1 = 675$

▶ Example: Multiply 65 by 67.

    $65 \times 67 = ?$
    $66^2 = 4,356$
    $4,356 - 1 = 4,355$

Multiplication Shortcut 10: Multiplying Two Numbers Four Digits Apart

A similar process is used for multiplying numbers four digits apart. First square the number exactly halfway between the two, and then subtract 4.

▶ Example: Multiply 25 by 29.

    $25 \times 29 = ?$
    $27^2 = 729$
    $729 - 4 = 725$

▶ Example: Multiply 65 by 69.

    $65 \times 69 = ?$
    $67^2 = 4,489$
    $4,489 - 4 = 4,485$

Division Shortcuts

Performing division problems is even more complex than multiplication and more difficult to envision in your head. However, a number of great shortcuts eliminate many of the problems of division calculations.

Division Shortcut 1: Fast Division by 4

This is a very straightforward shortcut. Just cut the number in half, and then cut the result in half again.

▶ Example: Divide 74 by 4.

$$74 \div 2 = 37$$
$$37 \div 2 = 18.5$$

If the decimal values are confusing, increase the number by 10 and then divide the final result by 10:

▶ $74 \times 10 = 740$
$740 \div 2 = 370$
$370 \div 2 = 185$
$185 \div 10 = 18.5$

Division Shortcut 2: Fast Division by 5

To quickly and easily divide by 5, first multiply the number by 2 and then move the decimal point one place to the left.

▶ Example: Divide 28 by 5.

$$28 \div 5 = ?$$
$$28 \times 2 = 56$$
56 converts to 5.6

▶ Example: Divide 412 by 5.

$$412 \div 5 = ?$$
$$412 \times 2 = 824$$
824 converts to 82.4

Division Shortcut 3: Fast Division by 25

A similar process is used to divide by 25. First multiply the number by 4 and then insert or move the decimal point two places to the left.

▶ **Example: Divide 230 by 25.**

230 ÷ 25 = ?
230 × 4 = 920
920 converts to 9.2

▶ **Example: Divide 470 by 25.**

470 ÷ 25 = ?
470 × 4 = 1,880
1,880 converts to 18.8

As with anything new, the more you practice these shortcuts, the more proficient you become.

LOOKING AHEAD

The next chapter concludes the incredible shortcuts section by examining many processes for conversion (among decimals, percentages, and fractions), measurements, and time shortcuts (e.g., how long it takes to double or triple a deposit based on a fixed interest rate).

C H A P T E R   1 2

Incredible Conversion, Measurement, and Time Shortcuts

A mong the valuable math shortcuts managers are likely to need are those involving conversions between different numerical systems, measurements, and fast estimates of time and yield. This chapter takes a look at these important areas.

CONVERSION

Converting from one system to another is often desirable. For example, it is easier to multiply decimal-based values than those expressed in fractions. Conversions among decimals, fractions, and percentages are inevitable in many business applications.

In an earlier chapter, the method for converting percentage to decimal was explained and expressed in two formats. First was the decimal shift:

$r.0\% = 00r.0 = 0.0r$ decimal

where: r = any percentage value

Second was the process of dividing a percentage by 100:

$r \div 100 = D$

The purpose of converting between systems usually is to make it easier to perform functions. For example, you can rapidly multiply by 75 with the use of fractions, using one of two methods. First, divide by 2, then add half of the result:

Multiplying by 75 Using Division

$[(V \div 2) \times 1.5] \times 100 = P$

where: V = value

   P = product

On a spreadsheet, enter the following:

A1   = SUM(V/2)
B1   = SUM(A1/2) + A1
C1   = SUM(B1*100)

▶ Example: Multiply 126 by 75.

$[(126 \div 2) \times 1.5] \times 100 = 9{,}450$

A second method involves the use of a fraction. The value 75 is equal to 3/4 of 100. So using this converted value, multiplying by 75 can be expressed in another way:

Multiplying by 75 Using a Fraction

$V \times 3/4 \times 100 = P$

where: V = value

   P = product

On a spreadsheet, enter:

```
A1    V
B1    SUM(A1*3/4)
C1    = SUM(B1*100)
```

▶ Example: Multiply 126 by 75 using the fraction 3/4.

$126 \times 3/4 \times 100 = 9,450$

BASIC MATH REVIEW

To multiply a whole number by a fraction, first multiply the whole number by the numerator of the fraction; then divide the answer by the denominator. For example: $(126 \times 3) \div 4 = 94.5$

Many functions are easier when converted from one system to another. For example, to convert fractions to decimals, divide the numerator by the denominator.

Converting a Fraction to a Decimal

$n \div d = a$

where: n = numerator
d = denominator
a = answer, decimal form

On a spreadsheet:

```
A1    N
B1    D
C1    = SUM(A1/B1)
```

▶ Example: Convert the fraction 3/4 to decimal form.

$3 \div 4 = 0.75$

This works with fractions of any size or complexity.

▶ Example: Convert the fraction 32/49 to decimal form

32 ÷ 49 = 0.653

You may also want to convert percentages to fractions. To do this, make the percentage the numerator and add a denominator that is one place greater than the whole number of the percentage—10, 100, 1,000, etc.

▶ Example: Convert 35% to a fraction. First, express it in fractional form.

35/100

Next, convert the fraction to the lowest common denominator. Both parts of the fraction are divisible by 5:

Numerator: 35 ÷ 5 = 7
Denominator: 100 ÷ 5 = 20

The value of 35% is equal to the fraction 7/20.

If the percentage is a fractional number, convert the fraction by multiplying both top and bottom by 10 for each decimal place.

▶ Example: To make 3.5 a whole number, multiply by 10:

3.5 × 10 = 35

If the fraction is less than a whole number, multiply the result by 10 for each decimal place.

▶ Example: Convert the percentage 0.35% to fraction form. First, express the percentage as a fraction: 0.35/100. Then multiply each side by 100 (two decimal places):

Numerator: 0.35 × 100 = 35
Denominator: 100 × 100 = 10,000

The percentage 0.35 is equal to the fraction 35/10,000, or 7/2,000.

▶ Example: Convert 3.5 to fraction form.

Express as a fraction: 3.5/100
Multiply each side by 10 (one decimal place):

Numerator: $3.5 \times 10 = 35$
Denominator: $100 \times 10 = 1,000$

The fractional equivalent of 3.5% is 35/1,000 or 7/200.

Performing basic math functions with fractions is not as simple as it is with whole numbers. To add fractions, the traditional method is to first find the common denominator and then to add the numerators. This can be tedious and difficult for complex fractions, but there is a valuable shortcut.

Adding Fractions

$$(n_1 \times d_2) + (d_1 \times n_2) = n_a$$
$$d_1 \times d_2 = d_a$$

where: $n_1 =$ numerator, first fraction
         $d_1 =$ denominator, first fraction
         $n_2 =$ numerator, second fraction
         $d_2 =$ denominator, second fraction
         $n_a =$ numerator, answer
         $d_a =$ denominator, answer

On a spreadsheet:

A1 N_1
A2 D_1
B1 N_2
B2 D_2
C1   = SUM(A1*B2) + (A2*B1)
D1   = SUM(A2 + B2)

► Example: Add the fractions 2/3 and 3/4.

Numerator: $(2 \times 4) + (3 \times 3) = 17$
Denominator: $4 \times 3 = 12$

The answer is 17/12, which can be next converted to a whole number with a fraction. This is necessary whenever the numerator is larger than the denominator. To make this conversion, subtract a whole number equivalent from the fraction, and then add the whole number to the result:

Subtract excess: $17/12 - 12/12 = 5/12$
Add the whole number: $1 (=12/12) + 5/12 = 1^5/_{12}$

To subtract fractions, the cross-multiplied fractions are subtracted from one another.

Subtracting Fractions

$$(n_1 \times d_2) - (d_1 \times n_2) = n_a$$
$$d_1 \times n_2 = d_a$$

where: $n_1 =$ numerator, first fraction
$d_1 =$ denominator, first fraction
$n_2 =$ numerator, second fraction
$d_2 =$ denominator, second fraction
$n_a =$ numerator, answer
$d_a =$ denominator, answer

On a spreadsheet:

A1 N_1
A2 D_1
B1 N_2
B2 D_2
C1 $= $ SUM(A1*B2)-(A2*B1)
D1 $= $ SUM(A2*B2)

► Example: Subtract 1/3 from 5/8. Let's call the larger fraction, 5/8, the first fraction.

$(5 \times 3) - (8 \times 1) = 7$ (numerator)
$8 \times 3 = 24$ (denominator)
$5/8 - 1/3 = 7/24$

To prove this outcome, check using the traditional method, in which both fractions are converted to their lowest common denominator; the numerators are subtracted:

$5/8 - 1/3 = 15/24 - 8/24 = 7/24$

Here are the steps involved:

1. *Convert to lowest common denominator.* Both sides of the fraction 5/8 are multiplied by three to arrive at 15/24. Next, both sides of the fraction 1/3 are multiplied by 8 to arrive at 8/24.
2. *The numerators are subtracted.* So 15 minus 8 $= 7$, and the answer is 7/24.

To multiply fractions, just multiply both numerators to find the top portion; then multiply both denominators.

Multiplying Fractions

$n_1 \times n_2 = n_a$
$d_1 \times d_2 = d_a$

where: $n_1 =$ numerator, first fraction
        $d_1 =$ denominator, first fraction
        $n_2 =$ numerator, second fraction
        $d_2 =$ denominator, second fraction
        $n_a =$ numerator, answer
        $d_a =$ denominator, answer

On a spreadsheet:

A1 N_1
A2 D_1
B1 N_2
B2 D_2

```
C1    = SUM(A1*B1)
D1    = SUM(A2*B2)
```

▶ Example: Multiply 1/3 by 5/8.

$1 \times 5 = 5$ (numerator)
$3 \times 8 = 24$ (denominator)
$1/3 \times 5/8 = 5/24$

To multiply mixed values—whole numbers with fractions—two methods can be used. First, convert the mixed number to a decimal equivalent. To do this, divide the numerator by the denominator and affix the decimal value to the whole number. Then repeat the step for the second value, and then multiply both values.

Multiplying Mixed Numbers with Conversion to Decimal Form

$$[(n_1 \div d_1) + w_1] \times [(n_2 \div d_2) + w_2] = a$$

where: n_1 = numerator, first value's fraction
d_1 = denominator, first value's fraction
w_1 = whole value portion, first part
n_2 = numerator, second value's fraction
d_2 = denominator, second value's fraction
w_2 = whole value portion, second part
a = answer

On a spreadsheet:

```
A1    N₁
A2    D₁
A3    W₁
B1    N₂
B2    D₂
B3    W₂
C1    = SUM(A1/A2) + A3
C2    = SUM(B1/B2) + B3
D1    = SUM(C1*C2)
```

▶ Example: Multiply $17^3/_4$ by $42^3/_8$.

$$[(3 \div 4) + 17] \times [(3 \div 8) + 42] = 752.15625$$

To divide fractions, the shortcut is to reverse the numerator and denominator of the first fraction, and then multiply by the second.

Dividing Fractions

$$d_1 \times n_2 = n_a$$
$$n_1 \times d_2 = d_a$$

where: n_1 = numerator, first fraction
d_1 = denominator, first fraction
n_2 = numerator, second fraction
d_2 = denominator, second fraction
n_a = numerator, answer
d_a = denominator, answer

On a spreadsheet:

A1	N_1
A2	D_1
B1	N_2
B2	D_2
C1	= SUM(A2*B1)
D1	= SUM(A1*B2)

▶ Example: Divide 5/8 by 1/3.

$8 \times 1 = 8$ (numerator)
$5 \times 3 = 15$ (denominator)
$5/8 + 1/3 = 8/15$

The solutions to working with fractions are methodical and logical. Learning and applying the methods to simple fractions demonstrates how they can be applied with equal ease to even the most complex fractions.

MEASUREMENTS

Managers may face situations in which measurements are necessary. They may have to find the area of a department as part of a proration for the annual budget, or they may have to calculate the area of a triangular piece of land owned by the company.

Many space measurements rely on the calculated value of *pi*. This lowercase Greek letter is denoted in formulas with the symbol π, which is the calculated sum of the circumference of any circle, divided by its diameter. The size of the circle does not vary because the calculation always results in the same answer.

Pi

$$C \div D = \pi$$

where: C = circumference of a circle
D = diameter of a circle
π = pi

On a spreadsheet:

```
A1    C
B1    D
C1    = SUM(A1/B1)
```

▶ Example: The circumference of a circle is 223 inches. Its diameter is 70.983 inches. Pi is equal to:

$$44.6 \div 14.2 = 3.1416$$

BASIC MATH REVIEW

The circumference of a circle is the distance around its entire area. *Diameter* is the distance from any point on the outside of the circle, through its exact middle, and to the opposite side.

Circumference of a Circle

$$\pi \times D = C$$

where: π = pi
$\quad\quad$ D = diameter
$\quad\quad$ C = circumference

On a spreadsheet:

A1 $\quad$ 3.1416
B1 $\quad$ D
C1 $\quad$ = SUM(A1*B1)

▶ Example: The diameter of a circle is 3 inches. The circumference is:

3.1416 × 3 inches = 9.425 inches

The most basic measurement is that of area for either a square or a rectangle. In both cases, length is multiplied by width.

Area of a Square or Rectangle

$L \times W = A$

where: $\quad L$ = length
$\quad\quad$ W = width
$\quad\quad$ A = area

On a spreadsheet:

A1 $\quad$ L
B1 $\quad$ W
C1 $\quad$ = SUM(A1*B1)

▶ Example: A square measures 14 by 14 feet. The area is:

14 feet × 14 feet = 196 square feet

▶ Example: A rectangle measures 16 by 25 feet. The area is:

16 feet × 25 feet = 400 square feet

If the measurement also includes inches, as an area often does, the entire formula should be converted to inches, multiplied, and then converted back to feet.

Area with Feet and Inches

$$\{[(F_1 \times 12) + l_1] \times [(F_2 \times 12) + l_2]\} \div 144 = A$$

where: F_1 = feet, first measurement
l_1 = inches, first measurement
F_2 = feet, second measurement
l_2 = inches, second measurement
A = area, in square feet and inches

On a spreadsheet:

A1 F_1
A2 l_1
B1 F_2
B2 l_2
C1 $= \text{SUM(A1*12)} + \text{A2}$
C2 $= \text{SUM(B1*12)} + \text{B2}$
D1 $= \text{SUM(C1*C2)/144}$

▶ Example: The rectangle you need to measure is 16 feet, 3 inches by 25 feet, 4 inches. The area is:

$$\{[(16 \times 12) + 3] \times [(25 \times 12) + 4]\} \div 144 = 411^2/_3$$

The fractional foot, 2/3, can be converted to inches as well:

$2/3 \times 12$ square inches $= 8$ square inches

The answer is that the area is 411 square feet and 8 square inches.

To compute the area of a circle, you need to first calculate the radius, which is one-half of the diameter. The diameter is a measurement from one side to the next, and the radius represents the distance from any outer point on the circle to its exact middle.

Radius

$D \div 2 = R$

where: D = diameter
R = radius

On a spreadsheet:

A1   D
B1   = SUM(A1/2)

To calculate the area of a circle, multiply the square of the radius by pi.

Area of a Circle

$R^2 \times \pi = A$

where: R = radius
π = pi
A = area of the circle

On a spreadsheet:

A1   R
B1   = SUM(A1*A1)*3.1416

▶ **Example: The radius of a circle is 5 inches. The area is:**

$5^2 \times 3.1416 = 78.54$

The area of triangles can also be calculated quite easily. No matter what type of triangle is involved (right angle, acute angle, or obtuse angle), the area is calculated in the same way.

Area of a Triangle

$(b \times a) \div 2 = A$

where: b = base
a = altitude
A = area

On a spreadsheet:

A1   B
B1   A
C1   = SUM(A1*B1)/2

BASIC MATH REVIEW

The *base* of a triangle is the measurement of its bottom line. *Altitude* is the distance between the base and the highest point. In calculations involving triangles, lowercase letters are used for calculating area, and uppercase letters are used for finding angles.

▶ Example: A triangle's base is 7 inches and its altitude is 4 inches. The area is:

(7 inches $\times$ 4 inches) $\div$ 2 = 14 square inches

The calculation of area for odd shapes involves variations and combinations of the basic formulas for the areas of rectangles and triangles. The odd shapes are broken down into a more easily calculated series of rectangles and triangles. The area of each is computed, and the areas' results are then added. For example, a trapezoid can be broken down into a rectangle and a triangle, or even into two triangles. After this, calculating area is relatively easy for each subshape.

A somewhat more complex formula applies when you need to calculate the volume of a rectangular solid.

Volume of a Rectangular Solid

$L \times W \times H = V$

where: L = length
         W = width
         H = height
         V = volume

On a spreadsheet:

A1   L
B1   W

```
C1    H
D1    =  SUM(A1*B1*C1)
```

▶ Example: Your company is going to store some items during a corporate move. You are comparing the storage capacity of three different
  storage units. You need to know the volume of each. They measure 9
  × 8 × 12, 10 × 12 × 8, and 12 × 14 × 10 feet. The volume of each is:

  9 × 8 × 12 = 864 cubic feet
  10 × 12 × 8 = 960 cubic feet
  12 × 14 × 10 = 1,680 cubic feet

The volume of a cylinder, such as a rural storage building, is more
complex because of its circular construction.

Volume of a Cylinder

$$R^2 \times \pi \times H = V$$

where: R = radius
        π = pi
        H = height
        V = volume of a cylinder

On a spreadsheet:

```
A1      R
B1      =  SUM(A1*A1)*3.1416
H =     =  SUM(B1*H)
```

▶ Example: A cylinder has a radius of 15 feet and is 25 feet high. The
  volume of this structure is:

  15^2 feet × 3.1416 × 25 feet = 17,671.5 cubic feet

TIME SHORTCUTS

The last variety of shortcuts involves calculations of how long it will take
to double or triple a sum of money left on deposit. These are estimates

based on an assumed rate of interest. The first is known as the *Rule of 72*.

Rule of 72

$72 \div i = Y$

where: i = interest rate
         Y = years required to double the fund

On a spreadsheet:

A1   I
B1   = SUM(72/A1)

▶ Example: Your company has set up a reserve for cash flow and has deposited a sum of $5,000 into stock that yields an annual dividend of 6%. How long will it take to double?

$72 \div 6 = 12$ years

Although the Rule of 72 is popular, a slightly more accurate variation is called the *Rule of 69*. In this formula, the same steps are involved as for the Rule of 72, but the value of 0.35 is added to the answer.

Rule of 69

$(69 \div i) + 0.35 = Y$

where: i = interest rate
         Y = years required to double the fund

On a spreadsheet:

A1   I
B1   = SUM(69/A1) + .35

▶ Example: Using the information from the previous example:

$(69 \div 6) + 0.35 = 11.85$ years (about 11 years, 10 months)

A third estimation is the *Rule of 113*, which quickly approximates the time required to triple a fund.

Rule of 113

$113 \div i = Y$

where: i = interest rate
Y = years required to triple the fund

On a spreadsheet:

A1   I
B1   = SUM(113/A1)

▶ Example: Using the information from the previous example of $5,000 on deposit at 6%:

$(113 \div 6) = 18.8$ years

These estimations are quite handy for comparing alternatives when money is going to be left on deposit. Like so many mathematical functions, any shortcut is useful if it saves time and improves accuracy. A shortcut can be used to rapidly calculate exact answers or to find the approximate answer. For any manager requiring the use of math—and that includes virtually all managers—being able to plug in a shortcut improves confidence and makes any task easier.

Summary of Formulas

Accumulated Value of a Series of Deposits

$$D\{[(1 + R)^n - 1] \div R\} = A$$

where: D = periodic deposit amount
R = periodic interest rate
n = number of periods
A = accumulated value

Adding Fractions

$$(n_1 \times d_2) + (d_1 \times n_2) = n_a$$
$$d_1 \times n_2 = d_a$$

where: n_1 = numerator, first fraction
d_1 = denominator, first fraction
n_2 = numerator, first fraction
d_2 = denominator, second fraction
n_a = numerator, answer
d_a = denominator, answer

After-Tax Return

$O \times (1 - T) = A$

where: O = operating (pretax) profit
T = combined federal and state tax rate (in decimal form)
A = after-tax profit

Amortization

$C \div M = A$

where: C = total cost
M = months to amortize
A = amortization per month

Annual Compounding

$(i + 1)^x \times P = D$

where: i = annual interest rate
x = number of years
P = principal deposited
D = total debt as of the number of years

Annual Percentage Rate (APR)

$[(\{[1 + (i \div p)]^n - 1\} \times L) + F] \div L = A$

where: i = interest rate
p = periods per year
n = number of periods
L = loan amount
F = fees
A = APR

Annual Straight-Line Depreciation

$B \div Y = D$

where: B = basis
Y = years in the recovery period
D = annual depreciation

Annualized Return

$(R \div H) \times Y = A$

where: R = return
H = holding period
Y = periods in one year (12)
A = annualized return

Area of a Circle

$R^2 \times \pi = A$

where: R = radius
π = pi
A = area of the circle

Area of a Square or Rectangle

$L \times W = A$

where: L = length
W = width
A = area

Area of a Triangle

$(b \times a) \div 2 = A$

where: b = base
a = altitude
A = area

Area with Feet and Inches

$\{[(F_1 \times 12) + I_1] \times [(F_2 \times 12) + I_2]\} \div 144 = A$

where: F_1 = feet, first measurement
I_1 = inches, first measurement
F_2 = feet, second measurement
I_2 = inches, second measurement
A = area in square feet and inches

Balance Sheet

$A = L + N$

where: A = assets
L = liabilities
N = net worth

Breakeven Return

$I \div (1 - T) = B$

where: I = inflation rate
T = effective tax rate, including both federal and state (in decimal form)
B = breakeven return

Cash Flow

$I + (N + L + A + S + O) - (L + A + S + D + O) = C$

where: I = net income
N = noncash expenses
L = loan transactions
A = capital asset transactions
S = legal settlements and judgments
O = other adjustments
D = dividends paid
C = cash flow

Cash Income

$I + D = C$

where: I = net income
D = depreciation expense
C = cash income

Cash-on-Cash Return

$C \div I = R$

where: C = net cash flow per year
I = initial cash investment
R = cash-on-cash return

Circumference of a Circle

$$\pi \times D = C$$

where: π = pi
$\quad\quad D$ = diameter
$\quad\quad C$ = circumference

Converting a Fraction to a Decimal

$$n \div d = a$$

where: n = numerator
$\quad\quad d$ = denominator
$\quad\quad a$ = answer, decimal form

Cost of Merchandise

$$B + M - E = C$$

where: B = beginning balance of inventory
$\quad\quad M$ = merchandise purchased
$\quad\quad E$ = ending balance of inventory
$\quad\quad C$ = cost of merchandise

Current Ratio

$$A \div L = R$$

where: A = current assets
$\quad\quad L$ = current liabilities
$\quad\quad R$ = current ratio

Current Yield on a Bond

$$N \div V = C$$

where: N = nominal yield
$\quad\quad V$ = current value of the bond
$\quad\quad C$ = current yield

Daily Compounding

$$[1 + (R \div i)^n] \times P = C$$

where: R = stated annual interest rate
      i = periodic interest rate (365 days)
      n = number of periods to be compounded
      P = principal
      C = compounded value

Daily Periodic Rate (365 Days)

$$R \div 365 = i$$

where: R = stated annual interest rate
      i = periodic interest rate (365 days)

Days' Sales Outstanding

$$R \div (S \div 365) = D$$

where: R = accounts receivable balance
      S = one year's sales on credit
      D = days' sales outstanding

Debt Coverage Ratio

$$I \div D = R$$

where: I = net income
      D = debt service
      R = debt coverage ratio

Debt Ratio

$$D \div T = R$$

where: D = long-term debt
      T = total capitalization
      R = debt ratio

Declining Balance (150%) Depreciation

$$[(B - P) \div Y] \times 150\% = D$$

where: B = basis
      P = previous years' accumulated depreciation
      Y = years in the recovery period
      D = annual depreciation

Declining Balance (200%) Depreciation

$$[(B - P) \div Y] \times 200\% = D$$

where: B = basis
       P = previous years' accumulated depreciation
       Y = years in the recovery period
       D = annual depreciation

Degrees of a Circle

$$P \times 360 = D$$

where: P = percentage of the total
       D = degrees

Dispersion Factor

$$\sqrt{v} \div [(V_1 + V_2 + \ldots V_n)] \div n = D$$

where: $\sqrt{v}$ = variance
       V_1 = first value in a field of values
       V_2 = second value in a field of values
       n = number of values in the field
       D = dispersion factor

Dividend Yield

$$D \div P = Y$$

where: D = dividend
       P = price per share
       Y = dividend yield

Dividing Fractions

$$d_1 \times n_2 = n_a$$
$$n_1 \times d_2 = d_a$$

where: n_1 = numerator, first fraction
       d_1 = denominator, first fraction
       n_2 = numerator, second fraction
       d_2 = denominator, second fraction

$$n_a = \text{numerator, answer}$$
$$d_a = \text{denominator, answer}$$

Earnings per Share (EPS)

$$E \div S = \text{EPS}$$

where: E = earnings
       S = number of common shares outstanding
       EPS = earnings per share

EBITDA

$$N - (I + T + D + A) = E$$

where: N = net income
       I = interest expense
       T = taxes
       D = depreciation
       A = amortization
       E = EBITDA

Equivalents in Multiplication

if $A = B$
and $A = C$
then $B = C$

where: A, B, and C = any values

Expense Variance

$$B - E = V$$

where: B = year-to-date budget
       E = year-to-date expense
       V = variance

Exponent (Used in EMA)

$$2 \div n = E$$

where: n = total number of values in the field
       E = exponent used in EMA calculation

Exponential Moving Average (EMA)

$$(\{V_p - [(V_1 + V_2 + \ldots V_n) \div n]\} \times (2 \div n)) + P = E$$

where: V_p = previous EMA
V_1 = first value in the field
V_2 = second value in the field
V_n = last value in the field
n = number of values in the field
P = previous EMA
E = new EMA

Fixed Asset Turnover

$$S \div [(B + E) \div p] = T$$

where: S = sales
B = beginning fixed asset value
E = ending fixed asset value
p = number of periods in the average
T = fixed asset turnover

Gross Margin

$$G \div R = M$$

where: G = gross profit
R = revenue
M = gross margin

Gross Profit

$$R - C = G$$

where: R = revenue
C = direct costs
G = gross profit

Half-Year Convention

$$C \div 2 = D$$

where: C = calculated full-year depreciation
D = depreciation, first year

Home Office Depreciation

$$\{[B \times (I \div A)] \div 27.5\} \times (of \div tf) = D$$

where:
B = basis (purchase price)
I = improvement value (assessed)
A = assessed value, total
of = office square feet
tf = total square feet
D = depreciation allowed

Income Statement

$$R - C = G$$
$$G - E = O$$
$$O - N = P$$
$$P - T = Z$$

where:
R = revenue
C = direct costs
G = gross profit
E = expenses
O = operating profit
N = nonoperating income or expense
P = pretax profit
T = income tax liability
Z = net after-tax profit

Inflation Rate

$$(C - P) \div P = I$$

where:
C = current CPI index
P = past CPI index
I = rate of inflation, CPI

Interest Coverage

$$E \div I = C$$

where:
E = EBITDA
I = interest expense
C = interest coverage

Inventory Turnover

$C \div [(B + E) \div p] = T$

where: C = cost of goods sold
B = beginning inventory
E = ending inventory
p = number of periods in the average
T = inventory turnover

Liability-to-Asset Ratio

$L \div A = R$

where: L = total liabilities
A = total assets
R = liability-to-asset ratio

Loan Amortization

$L \times [(R \times (P^n)] \div [(P^n) \times 1)] = A$

where: L = original balance of the loan
R = periodic interest rate (annual rate divided by periods per year)
P = present value of 1
n = number of periods (usually months)
A = required payment per period

Mean Absolute Deviation

$[(V_1 - A)^2 + (V_2 - A)^2 + \ldots (V_n - A)^2] \div n = D$

where: V_1 = first value in the field
A = average of the field
V_2 = second value in the field
V_n = last value in the field of n
n = number of values in the field
D = mean absolute deviation

Median

$(F \div 2) + 0.5 = M$

where: F = field of values
M = closest whole number to median

Midmonth Convention

$C(n \div 24) = D$

where: C = calculated depreciation
        n = monthly fraction
        D = first-year depreciation

Midquarter Convention

First quarter: $C[(1.5 \div 12] \times 7) = D$
Second quarter: $C[(1.5 \div 12] \times 5) = D$
Third quarter: $C[(1.5 \div 12] \times 3) = D$
Fourth quarter: $C[(1.5 \div 12] \times 1) = D$

where: C = calculated depreciation
        D = first-year depreciation

Monthly Compounding

$[(i \div 12) + 1]^x \times P = D$

where: i = annual interest rate
      x = number of months
     P = principal deposited
     D = total debt as of the number of months

Monthly Interest on a Loan

$I = B \times (i \div p)$

where: I = monthly interest
     B = balance forward
     i = annual interest rate
     p = number of periods in the year (usually 12 months)

Monthly Principal on a Loan

$P = M - I$

where: P = monthly principal
      M = monthly payment
      I = monthly interest

Monthly Straight-Line Depreciation

$B \div (Y \times 12) = D$

where: B = basis
       Y = years in the recovery period
       D = monthly depreciation

Multiplication by 0 and 1

$A \times 0 = 0$
$A \times 1 = A$

where: A = any value

Multiplication by 5

$(n \times 10) \div 2 = a$

where: n = number ending in 5
       a = answer

Multiplication by Even and Odd Values

$E_1 \times E_2 = E$
$E \times O = O$
$O_1 \times O_2 = O$

where: E = any even value
       O = any odd value

Multiplication of Positive and Negative Values

$P_1 \times P_2 = P$
$P \times N = N$
$N_1 \times N_2 = P$

where: P = positive value
       N = negative value

Multiplying by 75 Using a Fraction

$V \times 3/4 \times 100 = P$

where: V = value
 P = product

Multiplying by 75 Using Division

$[(V \div 2) \times 1.5] \times 100 = P$

where: V = value
 P = product

Multiplying Fractions

$n_1 \times n_2 = n_a$
$d_1 \times d_2 = d_a$

where: n_1 = numerator, first fraction
 d_1 = denominator, first fraction
 n_2 = numerator, second fraction
 d_2 = denominator, second fraction
 n_a = numerator, answer
 d_a = denominator, answer

Multiplying Mixed Numbers with Conversion to Decimal Form

$[(n_1 \div d_1) + w_1] \times [(n_2 \div d_2) + w_2] = a$

where: n_1 = numerator, first value's fraction
 d_1 = denominator, first value's fraction
 w_1 = whole value portion, first part
 n_2 = numerator, second value's fraction
 d_2 = denominator, second value's fraction
 w_2 = whole value portion, second part
 a = answer

Net After-Tax Profit

$P - T = Z$

where: P = pretax profit
 T = income tax liability
 Z = net after-tax profit

Net Return

$P \div R = N$

where: P = net profit
R = revenue
N = net return

Net Return on Equity

$P \div (E - S) = N$

where: P = net profit
E = equity (net worth)
S = redeemable preferred stock
N = net return on equity

New Balance Forward on a Loan

$N = B - P$

where: N = new monthly balance forward
B = balance forward
P = monthly principal

Operating Profit

$G - E = O$

where: G = gross profit
E = expenses
O = operating profit

Payback Ratio

$I \div C = R$

where: I = initial cash investment
C = net cash flow per year
R = payback ratio

Percentage Change

$(N - O) \div O = P$

where: N = new base value
O = old base value
P = percentage change

Percentage Conversion to Decimal

Decimal shift: $r.0\% = 00r.0 = 0.0r$
Divide by 100: $r \div 100 = D$

where: r = percentage rate
D = decimal equivalent

Percentage of Expense Variance

$V \div B = P$

where: V = year-to-date variance (favorable or unfavorable)
B = year-to-date budget
P = percentage of expense variance

Percentage of Revenue

$C \div R = P$

where: C = income statement component
R = revenue
P = percentage

Percentage of the Total

$V \div T = P$

where: V = value
T = total
P = percentage of the total

Periodic Rate

$R \div p = i$

where: R = nominal interest rate
p = number of periods
i = periodic interest rate

Pi

$$C \div D = \pi$$

where: C = circumference of a circle
          D = diameter of a circle
          π = pi

Present Value of a Single Deposit

$$\{1 \div [1 + (i \div p)]^n\} \times D = V$$

where: i = annual interest rate
       p = number of periods in the compounding method
       n = periods until the deposit amount is needed
       D = end-result deposit
       V = amount needed to be deposited today

Present Value per Period

$$W \times \{1 \div [1 + (i \div p)^n]\} \div (i \div p) = D$$

where: W = periodic withdrawal amounts
       i = annual interest rate
       p = number of periods in the compounding method
       n = periods until the deposit amount is depleted
       D = initial deposit required

Pretax Net Profit

$$O + (-) N = P$$

where: O = operating profit
       N = nonoperating
           income or
           expense (net
           income added,
           net expense
           deducted)
       P = pretax profit

Price/Earnings Ratio

$$P \div E = PE$$

where: P = price per share
E = EPS
PE = price/earnings ratio

Proof of Proration

$$P_a + P_b = V$$

where: P_a = prorated value of a
P_b = prorated value of b
V = value to be prorated

Proration

$$V[(a \div) a + b] = P_a$$
$$V[(b \div) a + b] = P_b$$

where: V = value to be prorated
a = proration base factor a
b = proration base factor b
P_a = prorated value of a
P_b = prorated value of b

Quarterly Compounding

$$[(i \div 4) + 1]^x \times P = D$$

where: i = annual interest rate
x = number of quarterly periods
P = principal deposited
D = total debt as of the number of periods

Quick Assets Ratio

$$(A - I) \div L = R$$

where: A = current assets
I = inventory
L = current liabilities
R = current ratio

Radius

$D \div 2 = R$

where: D = diameter
R = radius

Remaining Balance Percentage on a Loan

$R = N \div L$

where: R = remaining balance percentage
N = new monthly balance forward
L = original loan amount

Return on Cash Invested

$(S - P) \div I = R$

where: S = sales price
P = purchase price
I = cash invested
R = return on cash invested

Return on Equity

$P \div E = N$

where: P = net profit
E = equity (net worth)
N = return on equity

Return on Net Investment

$(S - P - C) \div I = R$

where: S = sales price
P = purchase price
C = costs
I = cash invested
R = return on cash invested

Return on Purchase Price

$(S - P) \div P = R$

where: S = sales price
P = purchase price
R = return on purchase price

Rule of 69

$(69 \div i) + 0.35 = Y$

where: i = interest rate
Y = years required to double the fund

Rule of 72

$72 \div i = Y$

where: i = interest rate
Y = years required to double the fund

Rule of 113

$113 \div i = Y$

where: i = interest rate
Y = years required to triple the fund

Semiannual Compounding

$[(i \div 2) + 1]^x \times P = D$

where: i = annual interest rate
x = number of semiannual periods
P = principal deposited
D = total debt as of the number of periods

Simple Average

$(V_1 + V_2 + \ldots V_n) \div n = A$

where: V = value
$1, 2$ = field number
n = last number in the field
A = average

Simple Interest

$P \times R = I$

where: P = principal
R = interest rate
I = interest

Sinking Fund Payments

$D \times (i \div p) \div \{[1 + (i \div p)]^n - 1\}) = V$

where: D = target deposit
i = annual interest rate
p = number of periods in the compounding method
n = periods until the deposit amount is needed
V = amount of periodic deposits required

Square of Any Number Ending in 1

$(n - 1)^2 + [n + (n - 1)] = n^2$

where: n = number to be squared

Square of Any Number Ending in 5

$t \times (n + 1) :25 = n^2$

where: t = 10's value of the number to be squared
n = number to be squared
$:$ = affix

Square of Any Number Ending in 9

$(n + 1)^2 - [n + (n + 1)] = n^2$

where: n = number to be squared

Squaring a Number

$n^2 = S$

where: n = any value
S = square of the value

Standard Deviation

$$\sqrt{v}$$

Subtracting Fractions

$$(n_1 \times d_2) - (d_1 \times n_2) = n_a$$
$$d_1 \times n_2 = d_a$$

where: n_1 = numerator, first fraction
$\quad\quad\;\; d_1$ = denominator, first fraction
$\quad\quad\;\; n_2$ = numerator, first fraction
$\quad\quad\;\; d_2$ = numerator, second fraction
$\quad\quad\;\; n_a$ = numerator, answer
$\quad\quad\;\; d_a$ = denominator, answer

Variance

$$\{[(V_1)^2 + (V_2)^2 + \ldots (V_n)^2] \div n\} - (V_1 + V_2 + \ldots V_n)^2 = VR$$

where: V_1 = first value in the field
$\quad\quad\;\; V_2$ = second value in the field
$\quad\quad\;\; V_n$ = last value in the field of n values
$\quad\quad\;\; N$ = number of values in the field
$\quad\quad\;\; VR$ = variance

Volume of a Cylinder

$$R^2 \times \pi \times H = V$$

where: R = radius
$\quad\quad\;\; \pi$ = pi
$\quad\quad\;\; H$ = height
$\quad\quad\;\; V$ = volume of a cylinder

Volume of a Rectangular Solid

$$L \times W \times H = V$$

where: L = length
$\quad\quad\;\; W$ = width
$\quad\quad\;\; H$ = height
$\quad\quad\;\; V$ = volume

Weighted Average

$$[I_1 \times (L_1 \div L_t)] + [I_2 \times (L_2 \div L_t)] = W$$

where: I_1 = interest rate, loan 1
L_1 = borrowed amount, loan 1
L_t = total of amounts borrowed
I_2 = interest rate, loan 2
L_2 = borrowed amount, loan 2
W = weighted average

Year-to-Date Budget

$$C + Y = B$$

where: C = current-month budget
Y = prior year-to-date budget
E = year-to-date budget

Year-to-Date Expense

$$C + Y = B$$

where: C = current month expense
Y = prior year-to-date expense
B = year-to-date expense

Index